SERIOUSLY
FUN FACTS
FOR CURIOUS KIDS

Mind-Blowing and Mega Interesting Trivia
About Science, History, Animals and More

ADAM COOLIDGE

WELCOME, ADVENTURER OF FACTS!

Do you love weird questions, amazing discoveries, and the kind of facts that make you go, "Wait - what?!"

Then you're in the right place.

This book is packed with **seriously fun and interesting facts** about all kinds of topics - **science, history, animals, the human body, space, plants, and more.** You'll read about glowing oceans, lost cities, real-life superpowers, and creatures that sound like they escaped from a video game.

Whether you're reading a little at bedtime or gobbling up a whole chapter at once, there's something new to discover on every page. And at the end of each chapter, you'll find quizzes, challenges, and mini-missions to keep your brain buzzing!

So get ready to explore. The world is way weirder, cooler, and more amazing than you ever imagined.

Let's go, curious mind!

TABLE OF CONTENTS

SCIENCE AND DISCOVERY

CHAPTER 1:
HUMAN BODY SUPERPOWERS –
DISCOVER YOUR HIDDEN ABILITIES

Your body is more powerful, more complex, and more surprising than you've ever imagined.

Take a deep breath. Wiggle your fingers. Blink your eyes. Each of those tiny movements involves bones, muscles, nerves, and brainpower working together in perfect harmony. And the best part? You don't even have to think about it.

But what if we told you your body is capable of even more than that? Some of these powers you've already experienced. Others are rare, but real. Scientists are still discovering what the human body can truly do. And it turns out, we might be superhuman after all. Let's explore just how extraordinary you really are!

———————————————— 👊 👊 👊 ————————————————

SUPER STRENGTH & SMART STRUCTURE

Your **skeleton** is an engineering masterpiece. Light enough to move easily, strong enough to lift and carry. The femur, or thigh bone, is the largest and strongest bone in your body. Pound for pound, it's tougher than concrete.

Your jaw muscle is one of the most powerful muscles in your body. With it, you can exert more than 200 pounds of force, enough to crack a tough nut without tools.

Every muscle and bone is shaped for performance: to walk, run, climb, and react in split seconds. Athletes build on this system, but everyone has it built in.

———————————————— 👊 👊 👊 ————————————————

INTERNAL THERMOSTAT

Humans don't need batteries or coolants. Your body maintains its temperature at around 98.6°F (37°C), no matter the weather. The *hypothalamus* in your brain keeps everything in balance.

- If it's too hot, you sweat. Evaporation cools you down.
- If it's cold, you shiver. Muscle movement produces heat.

Some people have trained their minds to help regulate this. Wim Hof, also known as **The Iceman**, uses breathing and focus techniques to survive extreme cold, even climbing icy mountains in shorts.

SUPERVISION, SORT OF

You might not have laser vision, but your eyesight is still incredible. You can distinguish over 10 million different colors, detect motion in microseconds, and see in 3D. Each eye contains more than 100 million light-sensitive cells, more than most high-end digital cameras.

Most people have three types of color-sensing cells in their eyes, but some rare individuals—often girls—have **a fourth kind,** which gives them **a super sense of color.** This power is called *tetrachromacy,* and it means they can see colors most people can't even imagine!

☝ ☝ ☝

LIGHTNING FAST REACTIONS

Your nervous system is your body's high-speed internet. Touch a hot stove? Your hand pulls away *before* your brain even says "Ouch!" Some signals in your body don't even wait for your brain—they take a shortcut through your spinal cord, like a secret fast lane. That's why your reflexes happen so quickly, **quicker than a blink,** in just 0.15 seconds!

Your nerve signals zoom through your body like lightning. They can travel at 268 miles per hour—that's nearly as fast as a race car on a Formula 1 track! It's like having a super-speed messaging system built right into your body.

☝ ☝ ☝

THE BRAIN: MORE THAN A SUPERCOMPUTER

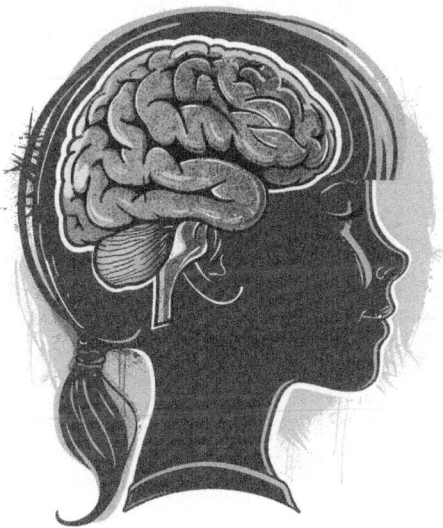

Weighing just about three pounds, your brain controls every breath, every step, every thought. And it never shuts off, even when you sleep.

Your brain is like the world's biggest library mixed with a super-powered computer. Scientists believe it can hold around **2.5 million gigabytes** of information, that's like watching cartoons non-stop for 300 years and still having room for more!

Need proof of its power?

- It can recognize a face in milliseconds
- It solves puzzles, imagines new worlds, and builds emotional memories.
- Even if part of your brain gets injured, it can rebuild and reroute its thinking paths, like a city making new roads after an earthquake. This amazing ability is called *neuroplasticity*. Think of it as your brain creating brand-new detours to keep working smoothly.

Some people train their memory like it's a superpower. They imagine a giant "mind palace" in their head, like a house with many rooms, where they store facts and numbers in each one. It sounds like magic, but it's a real way to remember huge amounts of stuff, just by picturing it.

Others learn to control pain, stress, and focus using nothing but thought. That's the power of your brain when you really pay attention to what it can do.

SELF-HEALING & CONSTANT REGENERATION

Your body is always fixing itself. Even while you sleep, cells are rebuilding:

- 25 million new cells per second
- Skin regenerates every 27 days
- Blood replaces itself every 3 to 4 months
- Your stomach lining rebuilds daily
- Your liver can regrow up to 70% of its mass

Break a bone? Your body sends in a repair team of cells that rebuild and sometimes strengthen it. No factory or robot in the world can self-repair this effectively.

MENTAL CONTROL OF THE BODY

The body and brain work as a team, and sometimes the brain takes charge in amazing ways.

- Buddhist monks can increase their skin temperature using only meditation
- Biofeedback experts can lower heart rates or manage pain without medicine

- People who are blind can learn echolocation—making clicks and "seeing" with sound like dolphins or bats

These powers aren't science fiction. They're real, measurable, and trainable.

———————— ✌ ✌ ✌ ————————

YOUR TONGUE IS A MAP OF SUPERPOWERS

You probably know your tongue can taste sweet, sour, salty, bitter, and umami (a savory flavor). But did you know that your taste buds grow back every 10 to 14 days?

That means your tongue is constantly refreshing itself, like a superhero recharging their powers! And some people, called **supertasters**, have way more taste buds than average. They can detect tiny differences in flavor that most of us miss.

So next time you grimace at a bitter veggie, don't worry: you might just be too powerful a taster.

———————— ✌ ✌ ✌ ————————

SOME PEOPLE CAN WIGGLE THEIR EARS—AND YOU CAN TOO

Only about **10–20% of people** can voluntarily wiggle their ears. Why? Because most of us have lost the reflex to move those muscles, but they're still there!

Some scientists believe these muscles are leftovers from our animal ancestors, who used them to aim their ears like radar dishes. With practice, some people can reactivate them.

It's not just a party trick: it's a reminder that your body still carries hidden abilities from deep in evolution's toolbox.

———————— ✌ ✌ ✌ ————————

SUPER STOMACH – ACID THAT CAN DISSOLVE METAL

Your stomach might be small, but it holds a chemical powerhouse. The acid inside your belly is called **hydrochloric acid**, and it's strong enough to dissolve razor blades and zinc metal in lab tests! (Don't eat those, though, your stomach isn't a superhero *on purpose*.)

So how do you survive your own acid? Your stomach grows a fresh layer of lining every few days to protect itself. It's like having a self-repairing force field that constantly regenerates.

That means your belly is a battle zone of digestion, powerful and protected.

Pretty awesome for something you never even see!

——————————— 🖐 🖐 🖐 ———————————

GENETIC SUPERPOWERS

Some people are born with rare traits that give them natural advantages, almost like they've got special upgrades hidden in their body's instruction manual. These traits come from tiny bits of information called *genes*, which work like a recipe, book for building you.

Here are some examples of real-life "genetic superpowers":

- **Muscle Boost:** A few kids are born with super-strong muscles, even without lifting weights.

- **Unbreakable Bones:** Some people have bones so dense and tough, they're hard to break, even in big accidents! Imagine having a skeleton made of superhero armor.

- **Super Sleep Saver:** A rare trait lets some people sleep just four hours a night and wake up feeling totally rested. Their body works like a super-efficient battery.

- **Mixed-Up Senses:** Ever heard music and seen colors at the same time? Some people do! It's called *synesthesia*, and it's like their brain's senses are talking to each other in secret.

Scientists study these rare abilities to understand how the body works—and maybe one day, use that knowledge to help others.

——————————— 🖐 🖐 🖐 ———————————

THE MYSTERIOUS SIXTH SENSE – REAL OR JUST BRAIN TRICKS?

Most people know the five basic senses: sight, hearing, smell, taste, and touch. But is that really all?

Some scientists believe we may have a "sixth sense" called *magnetoreception*: the ability to detect Earth's magnetic field, like some birds and sea turtles do. In a few experiments, people's brain waves reacted slightly when magnetic fields around them were changed. But here's the twist: no one noticed anything happening.

Does this mean humans have a hidden power they're not aware of? Maybe! But we don't know for sure. It's one of those wild scientific mysteries where the truth might be stranger than fiction. Even if you don't have a superpower compass in your head, your brain is definitely full of surprises.

QUIZ:
KNOW YOUR HIDDEN POWERS

1) What's the strongest bone in the body?

A) Spine

B) Femur

C) Skull

2) How fast can nerve signals travel?

A) 30 mph

B) 100 mph

C) 268 mph

3) What can your liver do?

A) Regrow itself

B) Beat like a heart

C) Control balance

4) How many gigabytes can the brain store?

A) 1,000

B) 2.5 million

C) 5,000

5) What is echolocation?

A) Hearing in 3D

B) Seeing without light

C) Using sound to locate objects

Answers: 1-B, 2-C, 3-A, 4-B, 5-C

🧪 TRY THIS! 🧪
CHALLENGE YOUR INNER SUPERPOWERS

Balance Challenge: Stand on one foot with your eyes open. Now close your eyes. Can you stay balanced? Your brain uses sight to help with posture—without it, things get tricky!

Breath Control: Take five deep, slow breaths. Can you feel your heart rate slowing down? You're using your brain to regulate your own body rhythm, just like monks and athletes do.

Reflex Test: Have a friend drop a ruler between your fingers. Catch it quickly. The shorter the drop before you grab it, the faster your reflexes!

Memory Snapshot: Look at a photo or illustration for 15 seconds. Now close your eyes and write down everything you remember. That's your visual memory at work.

◎BONUS CHALLENGE◎
INVENT A SUPERPOWER UPGRADE!

Design a new upgrade for the human body that boosts a real ability, like super-hearing, night vision, or mega memory.

Your mission:

- Choose a body function to enhance
- Name your upgrade
- Draw or describe how it works

Add a funny warning label (e.g., «Caution: May cause surprise backflips»)

Combine two upgrades to create **the ultimate human superhero!**

CHAPTER 2: WEATHER WONDERS – FROM FIRE RAIN TO ANIMAL FORECASTS

We all know the weather can change in a flash: sunny one moment, soaked the next. But sometimes, weather goes beyond unpredictable... it gets downright weird. Imagine a storm that rains frogs. Or a snowball that forms itself. What if the sky suddenly turned green, or fire started spinning like a tornado?

In this chapter, we're heading straight into the world of weather gone wild. These aren't made-up legends. Each phenomenon you'll read about really happened, and scientists are still trying to understand some of them.

So grab your umbrella—and maybe a lightning rod. Let's explore the wildest, strangest, and most unbelievable wonders of the weather world.

GREEN SKIES MEAN TROUBLE

When the sky turns green, take cover.

A greenish sky during daylight is often a sign that a severe thunderstorm is brewing, and possibly a tornado. Scientists think the color comes from sunlight interacting with moisture in the storm clouds, especially when hail is present.

It's not dangerous by itself, but it's nature's weird way of saying, "Something big is coming."

People across the U.S. Midwest have long associated green skies with the most violent weather.

CLOUDS THAT LOOK LIKE UFOS

They're not aliens—they're clouds!

Lenticular clouds are smooth, lens-shaped clouds that form when moist air flows over mountains. They hover in place and often look like stacked flying saucers, especially at sunset.

These clouds have fooled pilots and sky watchers for decades, and helped launch more than one UFO rumor.

FIRE TORNADOES ARE REAL AND TERRIFYING

It sounds like something from a superhero movie, but fire tornadoes (also called "firenadoes") are a real danger during wildfires.

A firenado forms when superheated air from a blaze begins to spin, pulling flames into a towering vortex. The result is a flaming twister that can leap into the sky and spread fire across entire landscapes.

One of the most powerful ever recorded occurred in California in 2018 and was strong enough to be rated an EF-3 tornado on the official scale!

THE WIND THAT SINGS

On certain nights, the wind doesn't just blow—it sings. The ancient Greeks believed it was the sound of gods or spirits. Scientists call it **aeolian tones**, after Aeolus, the mythological god of wind.

This eerie sound, sometimes described as whistling, humming, or even groaning, occurs when wind moves through caves, narrow canyons, or icy mountain passes. It creates natural wind instruments, turning rocks and air into a haunting concert.

LIGHTNING THAT TRAVELS 477 MILES

You already know lightning is powerful, but did you know it can be gigantic?

In 2020, scientists recorded a single lightning bolt that stretched 477 miles across Texas, Louisiana, and Mississippi. That's about the distance from New York City to Cleveland!

Called a **megaflash**, this type of lightning stays high in the atmosphere and spreads horizontally, often during supercell storms. It's not just long, it's also one of the brightest natural lights on Earth.

NATURE CAN MAKE ITS OWN SNOWBALLS

Ever seen a snowball rolling across a field—without a person in sight?

Meet the **snow roller**, a rare weather event where strong wind, just the right amount of sticky snow, and flat terrain create natural snowballs. The wind rolls up the snow like a cinnamon roll, forming hollow tubes.

Some snow rollers can be as big as car tires, and they've been spotted in places like Ohio, Canada, and Scotland.

ICE NEEDLES THAT GROW STRAIGHT FROM THE GROUND

Ever seen grass standing on tiny frozen stilts? In certain cold, damp conditions, water in the soil rises and freezes as it exits the ground, forming thin, delicate **ice needles** or **"frost flowers."**

These grow vertically from the soil, lifting small particles of dirt and sometimes even tiny pebbles. They can form overnight and melt just as fast when the sun hits.

Some look like spun glass or tangled hair, and are so fragile they vanish at a touch.

DUST DEVILS VS. TORNADOES

Dust devils may look like mini-tornadoes, but they're not born from storms.

They form on sunny, dry days when hot air near the ground rises quickly, spinning into a funnel of dust and debris. Most are harmless and short-lived, though they can toss lightweight objects or even cause minor injuries.

In 2016, a dust devil hit a trampoline in Colorado, and launched it 100 feet into the air!

YES, IT CAN RAIN FROGS (AND FISH TOO)

Throughout history, people have reported animals falling from the sky—and no, they weren't hallucinating.

When strong winds from waterspouts or tornadoes sweep across lakes or oceans, they can suck small animals (like frogs, fish, and even crabs) nto the air. These get carried along in storm clouds and sometimes fall dozens of miles away during a downpour.

In 2005, the town of Odzaci, Serbia, experienced a shower of frogs, startling residents and making headlines around the world.

WATERSPOUTS: TORNADOES ON WATER

Waterspouts look like oceanic twisters, and that's basically what they are.

They form when cold air moves over warm water, creating spinning columns of mist and spray. While weaker than land tornadoes, some waterspouts have capsized boats and launched fish into the air (which sometimes fall inland, as we learned earlier).

Sailors have feared them for centuries, calling them "sea devils."

🐾 🐾 🐾

SNOW THAT'S NOT WHITE AND SMELLS FRUITY

Snow is supposed to be white... right? Not always! In some high mountain regions, especially during summer, you might stumble across patches of snow that are bright pink or even red, and it smells like watermelon!

This bizarre sight is caused by a type of cold-loving algae called *Chlamydomonas nivalis*. When the snow melts just enough, these algae bloom and turn the snow pinkish-red. The snow even gives off a fruity scent, earning it the nickname **"watermelon snow."**

This phenomenon happens in places like the Sierra Nevada mountains in California, the Alps in Europe, and Antarctica. It's rare, but real, and surprisingly beautiful (Just don't eat it! Even though it looks fun, it can upset your stomach).

🐾 🐾 🐾

HEAT BURSTS: SURPRISE BLASTS OF HOT WIND

Ever felt a sudden gust of wind that's weirdly hot, even at night?

You might've experienced a heat burst. This rare event happens when cold air from a dying thunderstorm falls rapidly, compresses, and heats up just before hitting the ground.

Some heat bursts can raise temperatures by over 30°F (-1.1°C) in just minutes! In 1960, a heat burst in Kansas pushed the temperature to 136°F (57.9°C), one of the hottest ever recorded in the U.S.

🐾 🐾 🐾

BLOOD RAIN – WHEN THE SKIES TURN RED

It sounds like something from a horror movie, but blood rain is a real phenomenon! Several times throughout history, people have seen **red-colored rain** falling from the sky, especially in India, Europe, and the Middle East.

Scientists discovered that this eerie rain isn't actual blood, it's usually caused by **dust or algae** picked up by clouds and carried over long distances. When the rain falls, it's tinged red, orange, or brown, depending on what's mixed in.

Ancient people thought it was a sign from the gods or a bad omen. Today, we know it's just nature's strange chemistry trick.

ICE PANCAKES – THE BREAKFAST-LOOKING RIVER MYSTERY

In very cold rivers, large round disks of ice sometimes appear, gently spinning like lily pads. They're called **ice pancakes,** and they really do look like someone dropped a stack of frozen flapjacks in the water!

These frosty circles form when slushy ice clumps together and starts to spin in a slow current. As they bump against each other, their edges get rounded and raised, just like pancakes on a griddle.

It's a natural recipe whipped up by winter itself.

DOUBLE AND EVEN TRIPLE RAINBOWS EXIST

Rainbows happen when light bends through raindrops, but sometimes, you get a second (or third!) arc with reversed colors.

A **double rainbow** forms when sunlight reflects twice inside the water droplets. The second arc is usually fainter and flipped. Triple rainbows are extremely rare, but real—and even harder to photograph.

And yes, scientists have identified a **quaternary rainbow**, four arcs at once!

QUIZ:
WEATHER WONDERS

1) What causes a fire tornado?

A) Volcanoes

B) Spinning superheated air during wildfires

C) Lightning hitting a gas tank

2) What unusual thing happened in Odzaci, Serbia, in 2005?

A) It snowed in summer

B) Frogs fell from the sky

C) A rainbow lasted all day

3) What is a snow roller?

A) A snowplow

B) A sled

C) A naturally formed rolling snowball

4) Which type of lightning was nearly 500 miles long?

A) Cloud-to-ground

B) Megaflash

C) Bolt ball

5) What are lenticular clouds often mistaken for?

A) UFOs

B) Tents

C) Thunderheads

Answers: 1-B, 2-B, 3-C, 4-B, 5-A

⛈️ TRY THIS! ⛈️
BUILD A MINI WEATHER STATION

Want to predict the weather like a pro? Create a mini weather station to track what's happening right in your backyard!

You'll need:

A plastic bottle (for rain gauge), a straw and paper (for wind vane), a thermometer, paper and pencil.

What to do:

1. Cut the bottle to make a funnel-topped rain gauge. Mark measurements on the side.
2. Make a wind vane: tape a paper arrow to a straw and pin it on a pencil so it spins. Use a compass to mark directions.
3. Each day, check the wind direction, temperature, and rainfall—and write it down.
4. After a week, look for patterns. What changes when it rains? What direction does the wind blow before a storm?

Bonus: Name your station and give a weather report to your family!

🌪️ BONUS CHALLENGE 🌪️
STORM SURVIVAL SCENARIO

Time to choose: You're stuck in a wild weather situation. Pick one and explain what you'd do!

Would you rather...

? Be stuck on a boat during a waterspout OR be inside a car near a fire tornado? ?

Your job:

- Pick one scenario
- Defend your choice
- Create a quick "survival plan" or sketch of your response

Bonus: Create your own "Would You Rather" weather showdown and challenge a classmate!

CHAPTER 3: FUTURE TECH – ROBOT COOKS, SPACE ELEVATORS AND MORE

You may not see flying cars outside your window (yet), but the future is getting weirder (and cooler) by the minute.

Right now, scientists are building robots that can climb walls like geckos, machines that read your brainwaves, and even elevators that could one day take people into outer space. Some of tomorrow's tech is already here, quietly working behind the scenes. Other inventions are just blueprints... for now.

Will people one day live in underwater cities? Will your sneakers charge your phone as you walk? Can machines grow human organs? This chapter takes you on a ride through real inventions, wild predictions, and super-smart ideas that sound like science fiction, but might just be your future.

ROBOT CHEFS CAN COOK REAL MEALS

Meet your future kitchen helper: **the robot chef.**

In high-tech labs (and even some luxury homes), robot arms are being trained to cook full meals—chopping, stirring, flipping, and even plating—without a human touching a thing. One company has taught its robot to make beef stroganoff by watching videos of real chefs.

Some robo-chefs can learn just by observing cooking demos. Others follow a recipe stored in their software. You might not want one flipping pancakes just yet... but dinnerbots are on the way.

INVISIBILITY CLOAKS ARE ACTUALLY BEING TESTED

No, you won't be vanishing like a wizard just yet, but scientists are working on "metamaterials" that can **bend light around objects,** making them nearly invisible.

One version uses tiny crystals to redirect light, hiding small objects from sight. Another uses special cameras and screens to **mirror the background**, creating a cloaking effect.

It's still experimental, but it's not magic—it's physics. The real-life invisibility cloak might be closer than you think.

———————————— 🤖 🤖 🤖 ————————————

COMPUTERS THAT READ YOUR MIND – NO KEYBOARD REQUIRED

Typing with your fingers? That's so old-school. Scientists are developing **brain-computer interfaces** (BCIs) that let people control machines with their minds!

These futuristic headbands or implants read your brain signals and turn them into real actions. A person can move a robotic arm, control a cursor on a screen, or even type words, just by thinking. One system recently helped a person with paralysis send texts and play video games without lifting a finger.

It's not science fiction anymore—these tools are real and getting better every year. In the future, your thoughts might be the ultimate remote control.

———————————— 🤖 🤖 🤖 ————————————

THE HYPERLOOP – A TRAIN FASTER THAN A PLANE

Imagine a train that can move passengers at over **700 mph**, inside a sealed tube with no air resistance. That's the idea behind the **Hyperloop**, a futuristic transportation system being tested today.

Riding the Hyperloop might feel like flying, but on the ground! It could take you from Los Angeles to San Francisco in under 40 minutes.

If it works, the Hyperloop could change how we travel forever, and **make long-distance commuting as quick as a racecar lap.**

———————————— 🤖 🤖 🤖 ————————————

SCIENTISTS ARE BUILDING A SUN ON EARTH

The Sun creates energy through nuclear fusion, smashing atoms together at super-high temperatures. Now scientists are trying to do the same thing right here on Earth.

The project is called **ITER**, and it's building a fusion reactor in France that will heat hydrogen gas to over 150 million degrees Celsius, hotter than the core of the actual Sun. The goal? To create nearly limitless clean energy with zero pollution.

If it works, it could power the planet without oil, coal, or gas. A tiny artificial sun... that might save the world.

SOLAR PANELS THAT WORK AT NIGHT?

It sounds impossible—but scientists are working on special types of **"anti-solar" panels** that can **generate electricity even in the dark**!

How? Instead of absorbing sunlight, they use the heat difference between the Earth and the cold night sky to produce power. While they're not as strong as regular solar panels, they could be useful for remote areas or nighttime backup power.

The future might be filled with devices that harvest energy 24/7, even when the Sun's asleep.

⊙⊙⊙

SPACE ELEVATORS MIGHT REPLACE ROCKETS

Rockets are expensive, loud, and explode-y. What if we could reach space by... elevator?

It sounds like science fiction, but scientists are seriously working on building a **space elevator**: a super-strong cable that stretches from Earth into orbit. A solar-powered "climber" would carry people and cargo up the cable like a futuristic train, no rockets needed.

The biggest challenge? Finding a material strong enough to survive the trip. Carbon nanotubes or graphene might someday make it possible.

⊙⊙⊙

3D PRINTERS CAN BUILD HOUSE AND EVEN ORGANS

You've probably heard of 3D printing for toys or school projects. But now scientists are printing entire houses out of cement: layer by layer, faster and cheaper than using bricks.

Meanwhile, doctors are experimenting with special machines called *bioprinters* that might someday print skin, bones, and even hearts for patients who need new ones.

In the future, your doctor might not just treat your injury, they might print you a brand-new part! It's not just handy, it's life-saving tech, literally built from the ground up.

— 🤖 🤖 🤖 —

SELF-HEALING ROADS FIX THEIR OWN CRACKS

Potholes beware! Engineers in the Netherlands are testing asphalt that can heal itself.

They mix tiny pieces of steel wool into the road material. When cracks start to form, a special machine uses *induction heat* to warm the road and melt the cracks shut, without digging anything up.

This tech could save cities millions in repairs and give us roads that fix themselves before you even hit a bump. Smooth ride ahead!

— 🤖 🤖 🤖 —

SMART FABRICS CAN CHANGE COLOR AND CHARGE YOUR PHONE

Clothes that respond to your mood? Sneakers that power your tablet? These aren't fashion dreams: they're **smart textiles.**

Scientists are developing fabrics woven with tiny electronics. Some can change color based on temperature or light. Others generate electricity from body heat or movement, turning your jacket into a mini power plant.

Imagine charging your phone just by walking around in your hoodie. The future of fashion is more than cool—it's powerful.

— 🤖 🤖 🤖 —

TRASH-EATING ROBOTS CLEAN THE OCEAN

There's a robot that eats trash, and it loves snacks like plastic bags and soda bottles.

Meet **The Interceptor**, a solar-powered machine designed to float on rivers and gobble up plastic before it reaches the ocean. Other marine robots dive underwater and suck up oil spills or microplastic.

They don't just clean up messes—they're designed to work without hurting sea creatures, making them ocean-friendly heroes with mechanical stomachs.

— 🤖 🤖 🤖 —

ROBOBEES: TINY FLYING DRONES INSPIRED BY INSECTS

At Harvard University, researchers have created tiny flying robots that look like bees! These **"RoboBees"** have tiny wings that flap 120 times per second.

They could one day help with crop pollination, disaster search-and-rescue, or exploring places humans can't reach, like inside pipes or collapsed buildings.

Each RoboBee is smaller than a paperclip, but it carries a huge amount of science inside!

———————————— 🤖 🤖 🤖 ————————————

HOLOGRAMS YOU CAN TOUCH

We've all seen holograms in sci-fi movies, but now scientists are making **real holograms you can feel**! Using **ultrasound waves**, researchers can shape air pressure to make invisible objects that push against your skin.

It means you might someday high-five a hologram or play a piano made of light.

In the future, holograms won't just be for looking, they'll be for touching too.

———————————— 🤖 🤖 🤖 ————————————

SMART CONTACT LENSES

Scientists are developing **smart contact lenses** that do more than help you see. These futuristic lenses could one day measure your body's glucose levels, track your health, or even show you virtual data, like a screen floating in front of your eyes!

One company is even working on lenses that could help color-blind people see color.

In the future, your eyes might not just see the world, they could interact with it.

———————————— 🤖 🤖 🤖 ————————————

ROBOTS THAT CAN LEARN EMOTIONS

Robots aren't just stiff machines anymore. Thanks to **AI (artificial intelligence)**, some robots can now **detect human emotions** by reading facial expressions, body language, or tone of voice.

In Japan, a robot named **Pepper** can recognize joy, sadness, or anger, and even offer hugs or helpful suggestions. Some robots are being used in hospitals or schools to comfort patients and help kids learn.

It's not science fiction anymore. Robots are getting more human every day.

🧠 QUIZ: 🧠
TECH TIME CHALLENGE

1) What can robot chefs do?

   A) Eat pancakes

   B) Watch cooking videos and learn

   C) Grow vegetables

2) What is the biggest challenge in building a space elevator?

   A) Earth is too small

   B) There are no strong enough materials yet

   C) Nobody knows how elevators work

3) What is sticky, gray, and used by 3D printers to build houses?

   A) Bubblegum

   B) Robot glue

   C) Special cement

4) What do fusion reactors try to copy?

   A) Windmills

   B) The Sun's energy

   C) Volcanoes

5) What are scientists doing with brain organoids?

   A) Teaching them math

   B) Building tiny thinking robots

   C) Using them to study how real brains work

Answers: 1-B, 2-B, 3-C, 4-B, 5-C

⚙ TRY THIS! ⚙
FUTURE GADGET GENERATOR

What if you could invent a piece of future tech right now?

Here's how to build your own future gadget:

1. Pick a job your machine will do.
2. (Examples: clean your room, feed your pet, do your homework, braid spaghetti)
3. Decide what powers it:
   - Solar energy? Moonlight? Leftover pizza?
4. Choose what it's made of:
   - Recycled trash? Flexible plastic? Cactus juice?
5. Sketch it, name it, and explain how it works in 2–3 sentences.

Bonus: Write a warning label or slogan!

"Caution: May randomly sing opera while working."

🤖 BONUS CHALLENGE 🤖
REAL OR REALLY FAKE?

Time for a future-tech guessing game! Grab a friend and play:

1. Write down 3 real tech facts from this chapter
2. Invent 1 totally *made-up but believable one*
3. Mix them up and read them aloud
4. Can your friend guess which one is fake?

Example:

- A robot dog helps police
- A suit made of jelly lets you float in lava
- Moon dust can be turned into building bricks
- A mini brain in a dish grew tiny eyes

(Answer: yep, the jelly suit is fake... we hope.)

Switch roles and see who's the better future fact detective!

CHAPTER 4: OUTER SPACE ODDITIES – BIZARRE FACTS FROM BEYOND OUR WORLD

When you think of space, you might picture stars, planets, and astronauts, but the universe has far more surprises than most sci-fi movies. There are planets made of diamond, moons that smell like rotten eggs, and stars that spin hundreds of times per second like cosmic fidget spinners!

Outer space is vast—so vast, we haven't even scratched the surface of what's out there. But the things we *have* discovered are already incredibly weird, wildly wonderful, and sometimes just plain mind-blowing.

👾 👾 👾

GALACTIC CANNIBALISM – WHEN GALAXIES EAT EACH OTHER

Space isn't just big, it's hungry. Massive galaxies actually collide and devour smaller ones in a strange cosmic process known as galactic cannibalism.

Right now, our own **Milky Way** is slowly pulling in a nearby galaxy called the Sagittarius Dwarf Galaxy, stretching it apart and absorbing its stars. In a few billion years, the Milky Way will crash into its even larger neighbor, Andromeda, and the two will merge into a giant new galaxy!

Don't worry, stars are so far apart that most won't crash. But still... galaxy-eating? That's next-level weird.

👾 👾 👾

YOUR HEIGHT CHANGES IN SPACE

In microgravity, your spine stretches. That's why astronauts in orbit can **grow up to two inches taller** than they are on Earth!

The bones and muscles relax without gravity constantly compressing them. But when astronauts return home, gravity pulls everything back into place.

So technically, you can grow taller in space, but only while you're up there.

A PLANET THAT ORBITS IN JUST 18 HOURS

Most planets take months or years to orbit their star. But **Kepler-70b**, one of the fastest known exoplanets, zips around its sun in just 18 Earth hours!

That means a **year** on this planet is shorter than **one Earth day.** To make it even stranger, this planet is hotter than the surface of the Sun—over 12,000°F (6,800°C)—and is thought to be the remains of a former gas giant whose outer layers were blown away.

It's basically a super-speed, scorched world racing around its star like a cosmic bullet.

SATURN'S MOON THAT ACTS LIKE A MIRROR

There's a moon called **Enceladus** that orbits Saturn, and it's so icy and bright that it **reflects nearly all the sunlight** that hits it. In fact, Enceladus is one of the most reflective objects in the entire solar system!

Its surface is made of fresh, clean ice, and it even has geysers that shoot out water vapor from under its crust. Those frozen blasts constantly resurface the moon, like a planet giving itself a daily makeover!

Scientists think there may be a liquid ocean under all that ice, which makes Enceladus a top place to look for alien life hiding beneath a shiny shell.

A DAY THAT'S LONGER THAN A YEAR

On Venus, time plays tricks. A single day on this hot, cloud-covered planet lasts **243 Earth days**, but a full orbit around the Sun (its year) takes only 225 Earth days. That means one day is longer than one year!

Venus also spins backward compared to most planets, and its atmosphere is so thick it traps heat like a pressure cooker. Surface temperatures soar to over 860°F (460°C) —hot enough to melt lead.

So even though it's beautiful and bright in the night sky, Venus is one of the most hostile places in our solar system.

THE PLANET THAT SPINS SIDEWAYS

Most planets spin upright like tops. But not Uranus. This icy giant is tipped on its side so far, it **rolls around the Sun** like a bowling ball!

Scientists think a massive collision knocked it over billions of years ago. As a result, Uranus has super long, super weird seasons: each pole spends about 42 years in sunlight, then 42 years in total darkness.

———— 👀 👀 👀 ————

ALIEN RAIN – IT DOESN'T ALWAYS FALL AS WATER

Rain on Earth is wet and ordinary... but on other planets? Not even close.

- On Venus, it rains sulfuric acid, but the surface is so hot, the drops evaporate before they hit the ground.
- On Neptune, scientists think it rains liquid diamonds deep inside its atmosphere.
- And on Titan, Saturn's largest moon, it rains methane, a gas that's flammable on Earth!

Space weather isn't just strange—it's completely otherworldly.

———— 👀 👀 👀 ————

A PLANET THAT FLOATS

You know how heavy a planet must be, right? But here's a weird one: the planet Saturn is so light for its size that if you could drop it into a bathtub big enough (a really big one!), it would float.

Saturn is mostly made of gas, with a small core and super-low density. So while it's huge, it could fit over 750 Earths inside; it's the **lightweight champion** of the solar system.

———— 👀 👀 👀 ————

THE MOON THAT SMELLS LIKE ROTTEN EGGS

If you could land on **Io**, one of Jupiter's largest moons, the first thing you'd notice would be the smell. It's packed with volcanoes that constantly erupt sulfur, which smells like rotten eggs or burned matches.

Io is the most volcanically active place in our solar system. Some eruptions shoot lava and gases hundreds of miles into space. Its surface is a colorful patchwork of yellows, reds, and whites, like a pizza gone wrong.

A PLANET THAT MIGHT BE MADE OF DIAMONDS

Far beyond our solar system lies a mysterious exoplanet called **55 Cancrie**. It's about twice the size of Earth and may be made largely of carbon. Under the extreme pressure and heat of its atmosphere, scientists believe that carbon could crystallize into **diamond**.

This planet orbits so close to its star that its year lasts only 18 hours. Temperatures on one side soar to over 3,632°F (2,000°C).

It's beautiful, dangerous, and probably the universe's most expensive rock.

THE STAR THAT RINGS LIKE A BELL

In deep space, there's a white dwarf star known as PG 1159-035 that actually **vibrates** like a giant bell. We can't hear it, but astronomers detect its vibrations as changes in brightness.

These gentle starquakes can tell scientists about the star's temperature, age, and what it's made of—just like tapping a bell can tell you if it's hollow or solid.

It's cosmic music, even if we can't dance to it.

STARS THAT SPIN 700 TIMES A SECOND

When huge stars collapse, they sometimes become **neutron stars**: ultra-dense objects that can spin incredibly fast. Some of these, called **pulsars**, rotate up to **700 times every second.**

Each spin sends out beams of radiation, like a flashing cosmic lighthouse. They're so regular, scientists once thought the first pulsar signals were alien messages.

If Earth had a spinning top like that, it would blur out of existence!

ROGUE PLANETS – LOST WORLDS WITH NO SUN

Some planets are **completely alone**, floating through space **with no star to orbit**. They're called **rogue planets**, and scientists believe there could be **billions** of them in our galaxy.

These mysterious worlds may have been kicked out of their star systems long ago or formed in deep space all by themselves. Imagine a frozen planet drifting in total darkness, untethered, unknown, and possibly home to life forms that never see light.

They're the **loneliest travelers in the universe.**

———————————— 👀 👀 👀 ————————————

BLACK HOLES: TIME-BENDING, SPACE-STRETCHING MONSTERS

Black holes are the strangest things in the universe (and maybe the scariest). Get too close, and you won't just fall in. You'll fall into a whole new set of rules.

First, they mess with **time**. Near the edge of a black hole, known as the event horizon, gravity is so intense that **time actually slows down**. You could spend just one hour near it... and come back to find **years** have flown by on Earth! It's like a real-life time machine—no wires, no buttons, just physics.

Then comes the weirdest ride of all: **spaghettification**. That's the real word scientists use to describe what happens if you fall in. The black hole pulls so hard on your feet and your head that it stretches you into a long, thin noodle.

Yup, space pasta. Deliciously terrifying!

———————————— 👀 👀 👀 ————————————

THE TOUGHEST ANIMAL SURVIVED SPACE

Tardigrades, or water bears, are microscopic animals with incredible survival skills. They can survive extreme temperatures, radiation, and even the vacuum of space.

In 2007, scientists launched them into space **without any protection.** They were exposed to solar radiation, zero pressure, and freezing cold—and they survived.

These micro-marvels are about the size of a grain of salt, and yet they could outlast almost anything on Earth, or beyond it.

QUIZ:
SPACE IT OUT

1) Which planet spins sideways like a rolling ball?

A) Neptune

B) Uranus

C) Mercury

2) What does Jupiter's moon Io smell like?

A) Fresh lemons

B) Sulfur

C) Cinnamon

3) What kind of animal survived space?

A) Gecko

B) Tardigrade

C) Mouse

4) What happens to astronauts' height in space?

A) They shrink

B) They grow taller

C) They stay the same

5) Which star type spins hundreds of times per second?

A) Supernova

B) Red giant

C) Pulsar

Answers: 1-B, 2-B, 3-B, 4-B, 5-C

🪐 TRY THIS! 🪐
BUILD YOUR OWN PLANET!

You're the creator of a brand-new planet. What will it be like?

Write about your invented world. Include:

- Its name
- Size and color
- What kind of star it orbits
- Weather, atmosphere, gravity
- Any moons or rings
- One strange feature that makes it unforgettable!

Will it be a jungle-covered lava planet? A world made of ice and diamonds? Or something even weirder?

👽 BONUS CHALLENGE 👽
ALIEN COMMUNICATION MISSION

Aliens have landed—but they don't speak human languages! Your challenge:

- Create a message for them using only **shapes, pictures, sounds, or gestures**
- Try acting it out, drawing it, or recording it (no words allowed!)
- Ask a friend or family member to decode what you're trying to say (Is it "peace"? "Follow me"? "Don't eat me"?)

Reverse roles—can they make a reply using alien communication?

ANIMALS AND NATURE

CHAPTER 5: CREEPY, CRAWLY, AND TOTALLY COOL — INSECT & REPTILE FACTS

They slither. They buzz. They hiss and crawl. Insects and reptiles might be some of the least loved animals in the world—but they're also some of the most incredible.

There are insects that farm, snakes that play dead and lizards that shoot blood from their eyes. Weird? Yes. But also fascinating.

Reptiles and insects are some of the oldest creatures on Earth: millions of years older than humans. And during all that time, they've developed tricks that would make superheroes jealous. Get ready to squirm, gasp, and say "wow!" as we dive into some of the strangest, coolest, and most surprising facts about bugs and reptiles!

———————————— 🦗🦗🦗 ————————————

CROCODILES CAN'T STICK OUT THEIR TONGUES

Here's one you can test at your next zoo trip: crocodiles cannot stick out their tongues.

Why? Their tongues are held in place by a membrane that keeps them glued to the bottom of their mouths. It helps them keep their mouths open underwater without swallowing water.

Good thing, too. Imagine a crocodile with a lolling tongue—not quite as scary.

———————————— 🦗🦗🦗 ————————————

CICADAS: INSECT TIME TRAVELERS

Some insects take their time. A lot of time. The **periodical cicada** spends 17 years underground, then comes out in massive swarms.

They tunnel up by the millions, covering trees and making a huge, buzzing sound. Their plan? Overwhelm predators with numbers so some survive to mate and lay eggs. Then their babies go back underground, and the cycle starts all over again.

Would you wait 17 years for your big moment? These bugs do it without complaint.

LIZARDS THAT CRY BLOOD

The Texas horned lizard has one of the weirdest self-defense moves in the animal kingdom: it can **squirt blood from its eyes.**

When a predator (like a coyote) gets too close, the lizard builds up pressure in tiny blood vessels around its eyes—then suddenly blasts a stream of blood up to 5 feet! The blood not only surprises predators—it also tastes bad, which is great if you're a snack-sized reptile trying to escape lunch.

It's a defense strategy that's part superhero move and part horror film. Who knew eyeballs could be so powerful?

———————— ⒬⒬⒬ ————————

COCKROACHES: SQUISH-PROOF SURVIVORS

If there's one bug that's tough as nails, it's the cockroach. These tiny tanks can survive being stepped on, squashed, or squished, and they just keep crawling.

Cockroaches can squeeze their bodies through gaps as thin as a coin. Even more amazing, they can survive being crushed by pressure that's 900 times their own body weight. That's like a human being squashed by an elephant, and walking away from it.

Because of this, scientists study cockroach bodies to design small rescue robots that could crawl through earthquake rubble. Gross? Maybe. Genius? Definitely.

———————— ⒬⒬⒬ ————————

LEAF INSECTS THAT FOOL EVERYONE

Camouflage in nature isn't just smart—it's essential. And some insects take it to the next level by becoming the thing they're hiding on.

The Malaysian walking leaf doesn't just look like a leaf—it moves like one, too. It sways gently as it walks, as if blown by the wind. Its body has leaf-like veins, ragged edges, and perfect coloring.

To a hungry bird or lizard, it's just another leaf in the forest. And that's exactly what keeps it alive.

———————— ⒬⒬⒬ ————————

ANTS THAT HERD AND FARM

You may think humans invented farming, but ants were growing food long before we were.

Some ants "herd" tiny insects called aphids, which suck plant juices and leave behind sweet honeydew. The ants protect them, move them around, and "milk" them for food, just like we do with cows.

Leafcutter ants collect leaves, chew them up, and use them to grow a special fungus underground. The ants don't eat the leaves: they eat the fungus that grows on them. It's a miniature farming operation, complete with workers and garden caretakers.

———————————— @@@ ————————————

THE TURTLE THAT BREATHES THROUGH ITS BUTT

Yes, you read that correctly. The **Fitzroy River turtle** in Australia can absorb oxygen through its rear end. It uses this strange system to stay underwater longer during the dry season, up to 21 hours without coming up for air.

Scientists call it cloacal respiration. Kids (and everyone else) call it weirdly awesome.

———————————— @@@ ————————————

THE BEETLE THAT SHOOTS BOILING CHEMICALS

The **bombardier** beetle is one of the coolest creatures in the bug world, and one of the most explosive.

When attacked, it blasts out a **chemical spray that reaches 212°F (100°C)**—the temperature of boiling water! The beetle mixes two special chemicals in a tiny chamber inside its body. When they combine—BOOM!—a loud pop and a puff of hot, stinky gas send predators running.

This blaster is safe for the beetle but terrifying for attackers. It's like having a built-in bug-sized fire extinguisher... or a chemical cannon.

———————————— @@@ ————————————

GECKOS: MASTERS OF THE MICRO-GRIP

How do geckos walk on ceilings without falling? It's not magic: it's millions of tiny hairs.

Each gecko toe is covered in microscopic hairs, which split into even tinier tips. These tips form invisible connections with the surface they touch, creating a super-strong grip through a force called van der Waals interaction.

This lets geckos dash up walls, hang upside down, and even walk across glass. Scientists have tried to copy their foot tech to make gloves for real-life wall climbers!

———————————————— @@@ ————————————————

INSECTS THAT HEAR WITH THEIR KNEES

Crickets, katydids, and some grasshoppers don't have ears like ours, but they can still hear.

Their "ears" are actually on their legs, right below the knees. These special patches sense vibrations and allow them to detect danger, mates, or rivals nearby.

Hearing with their legs lets them stay super alert to danger. If a bird flaps nearby or another bug chirps a challenge, their knees can "listen" and respond fast. It's a survival trick that works from grasslands to jungles.

———————————————— @@@ ————————————————

THE CHAMELEON THAT ISN'T HIDING

People think chameleons change color to hide. Actually, they change color mostly to communicate.

When a chameleon is angry or showing off, it might turn bright red or yellow. When it's relaxed or trying to cool down, it might turn green or pale.

Their skin contains special cells that reflect light differently depending on mood and temperature, not just camouflage.

———————————————— @@@ ————————————————

MILLIPEDES THAT GLOW IN THE DARK

Meet the **Motyxia millipede,** a spooky crawler that **glows in the dark**. It lives in California and emits a soft, bluish-green light from its skin.

But this glow isn't for fun: it's a warning. The light tells predators, "I'm toxic! Don't eat me!" Scientists have confirmed that glowing millipedes are more likely to be left alone by predators.

In the world of bugs, sometimes the brightest lights come with the biggest warnings.

———————————————— @@@ ————————————————

MOTHS THAT JAM BAT RADAR

Bats hunt moths using **echolocation**, like natural sonar. But one clever moth has a counterattack: it **jams the bat's signal!**

The **tiger moth** can flap special organs to make ultrasonic clicks that confuse bats, making the moth harder to track or hit. It's like a **stealth jet with radar scramblers,** but fuzzier.

This defense is so effective, some bats even learn to avoid the sound altogether!

———————————————— ෴෴෴ ————————————————

SNAKES THAT GLIDE LIKE AIRPLANES

Some snakes don't need wings to fly. **Flying snakes**, found in Southeast Asia, can launch from trees and **glide through the air for over 100 feet!**

They flatten their bodies, wiggle in a wave-like motion, and use their ribs to "steer" midair. Scientists say they move like living boomerangs.

They don't fly to escape danger—they do it to hunt or move between trees. Who needs a plane when you've got built-in glider mode?

———————————————— ෴෴෴ ————————————————

THE CENTIPEDE WITH POISON CLAWS

Centipedes are already creepy with all those legs, but one kind, the giant Amazonian centipede, takes things up a level: it has venomous fangs... on its head!

These "fangs" are actually modified front legs that inject venom into prey. They're strong enough to take down insects, frogs, lizards, even mice and birds!

The centipede moves fast, coils around its victim, and stabs repeatedly like a tiny, slithery horror movie monster. It's creepy, crawly, and totally hardcore.

———————————————— ෴෴෴ ————————————————

THE SPIDER THAT CATAPULTS ITS PREY

Most spiders wait for insects to land in their web, but the ogre-faced spider doesn't wait around. It uses its web like a slingshot.

This night-hunting spider spins a stretchy square of silk, holds it between its front legs, and then pulls it back like a net. When prey walks by, it springs forward at lightning speed, throwing the web over its target with perfect aim.

It's like a spider doing a ninja net ambush—and it never misses.

QUIZ:
CREEPY, CRAWLY, AND TOTALLY COOL

1) What lets geckos climb up walls?

A) Suction cups

B) Gluey feet

C) Microscopic hairs

2) Which animal can breathe through its behind?

A) Spider

B) Turtle

C) Ant

3) How long do periodical cicadas live underground before emerging?

A) 7 years

B) 17 years

C) 27 years

4) What amazing defense does a bombardier beetle have?

A) It sprays boiling chemicals

B) It jumps like a flea

C) It glows in the dark

5) What does the Texas horned lizard do when threatened?

A) Changes color

B) Shoots blood from its eyes

C) Runs in circles

Answers: 1-C, 2-B, 3-B, 4-A, 5-B

TRY THIS!
DESIGN A SUPER CREATURE

Now that you've learned about exploding ants, sticky geckos, and beetles with chemical sprays—it's your turn!

Your challenge:

- Invent your own insect or reptile superhero by mixing 3 real abilities from this chapter.
- What powers will it have?
- How does it defend itself or find food?
- What does it look like?

Draw your creature and give it a name. Bonus: write a sentence about where it lives and what makes it totally cool (or creepy)!

BONUS CHALLENGE
CRAWL-OFF SHOWDOWN

Choose two creatures from this chapter and imagine they're facing off in a **friendly contest**—not a fight, but a talent showdown!

- Which animal would win in a climbing race?
- Who's sneakier?
- Who has the weirdest superpower?

Write a "commentary" like a sportscaster or judge the contest like a talent show. Add points for style, defense, and weirdness!

CHAPTER 6: SECRETS OF THE PLANT KINGDOM – WEIRD, WILD & LEAFY

Plants are everywhere: in gardens, parks, forests, and even your salad bowl. But don't be fooled by their quiet, leafy appearance. The plant kingdom is bursting with wild wonders! Some plants explode, others hunt, and a few can even move like animals. From trees that clone themselves to flowers that stink like rotten meat, plants are full of secrets just waiting to be discovered.

So get ready to meet nature's green geniuses. These plants are stranger (and sometimes sneakier) than you ever imagined. And the more you learn, the more you'll realize—plants are anything but boring.

THE PLANT THAT TELLS TIME

The **telegraph plant** (Desmodium gyrans) moves its leaves in a rhythmic pattern, almost like it's waving. Even without wind or touch, its side leaves twitch in tiny circles, especially in sunlight.

Scientists believe it's reacting to the time of day and sunlight levels. It even speeds up if you play music!

A dancing plant with a built-in clock? That's nature's choreography. Some people even grow it at home just to watch it groove.

THE LOTUS SEED THAT WAITED 1,000 YEARS

In China, scientists found a **lotus seed** in a dry lakebed. They planted it, and it **sprouted**, even though it was over **1,000 years old**!

Lotus seeds can stay dormant for centuries, waiting for just the right moment to grow.

That's one seriously patient plant. Its resilience has made the lotus a symbol of rebirth in many cultures.

THE PLANT THAT MAKES YOU FORGET EVERYTHING

In India, there's a plant called the **Dhatura**, also known as the **zombie cucumber**. It's so dangerous that even touching or smelling it can mess with your memory.

People who accidentally consume it (or are tricked into it) can experience **temporary amnesia,** confusion, and wild hallucinations—some can't even remember who they are for days. In ancient times, it was used in potions or poisons. Today, it's carefully studied for its powerful chemicals.

It's beautiful, but **absolutely brain-bending.**

꘎ ꘎ ꘎

TREES THAT COMMUNICATE UNDERGROUND

Trees in forests aren't just standing silently, they're **talking underground** through a network of fungi known as the **"Wood Wide Web."**

Through their roots, trees send signals, nutrients, and warnings. If one tree is attacked by insects, it can signal nearby trees to activate defenses.

It's like the internet, but made of roots and fungus. And yes, it's real. Some mother trees even feed nutrients to their "children."

꘎ ꘎ ꘎

THE PLANT THAT EATS BUGS

The **Venus flytrap** may look like it belongs in a sci-fi movie, but it's very real. Found in North and South Carolina, this plant has jaw-like leaves that snap shut when a bug lands inside.

It doesn't happen by accident. The flytrap has tiny hairs inside its trap. If a bug touches two hairs within 20 seconds, SNAP! The trap closes, and the plant slowly digests its meal.

Talk about a salad that bites back! It only takes a few days to digest its prey, and then the trap resets, ready for its next victim.

꘎ ꘎ ꘎

PLANTS THAT EXPLODE

Some plants don't wait around for animals to spread their seeds. They launch them like tiny missiles!

The **sandbox tree**, nicknamed the "Dynamite Tree," can explode with a bang loud enough to scare birds. Its seed pods burst open and fire seeds at over 100 miles per hour!

In another example, the **squirting cucumber** shoots out its seeds in a jet of slimy goo. If you thought plants were peaceful, think again.

There's even a plant in Africa called the **Devil's Claw**, whose seedpods have hooked claws that latch onto animal fur for a bumpy ride.

———————————— 🐜 🐜 🐜 ————————————

THE TREE THAT WALKS (SORT OF)

Deep in the Amazon rainforest, there's a legend about a tree that **walks**. The **Socratea exorrhiza**, also known as the **walking palm**, appears to move across the forest floor, very slowly.

It doesn't grow legs, of course. But it sends out new roots in the direction of sunlight and **abandons old ones**, allowing it to shift position over time. Some scientists debate if it really moves much, but it sure looks like a tree on a journey.

Even if it doesn't march like a robot, it's still one of nature's strangest illusions.

———————————— 🐜 🐜 🐜 ————————————

ZOMBIE FUNGUS THAT CONTROLS ANTS

Deep in the jungle, a creepy fungus called **Ophiocordyceps** takes over ants' brains. Once infected, the ant leaves its colony, climbs up a leaf, and clamps down, then the fungus grows **right out of its head!**

The spores rain down onto other ants below, spreading the infection.

It's not technically a plant, but it lives in the plant kingdom's world and behaves like something out of a horror movie. Some scientists believe there are different species of this fungus for different insect targets. Nature is terrifying—and clever.

———————————— 🐜 🐜 🐜 ————————————

PLANTS THAT GLOW IN THE DARK

Some mushrooms (which are fungi, but still closely related to plants) give off an eerie green glow at night. This is called **bioluminescence**, and it helps attract insects to spread their spores.

The phenomenon is called "foxfire," and it's been reported in forests for centuries. Some cultures used glowing wood as natural lanterns!

Scientists are even experimenting with glowing plants for natural streetlights in the future.

A TREE THAT CLONES ITSELF

Meet Pando, a massive grove of quaking aspens in Utah. It looks like a forest, but it's actually **one single organism!**

All of the "trees" are part of the same root system, and scientists believe Pando is at least **80,000 years old**, possibly more. That makes it one of the **oldest living things on Earth.**

It's a forest that's really just one super plant! And although it seems healthy above ground, Pando is actually shrinking because young sprouts are being eaten by deer before they can grow.

A TREE THAT SENDS CHEMICAL WARNINGS

In the African savanna, acacia trees are in constant danger of being munched by giraffes. But they've developed a **secret communication system**: using **smells**!

When a giraffe starts chewing, the acacia releases a chemical gas into the air. Nearby trees detect it and quickly **pump bitter toxins** into their leaves to make them taste awful. Giraffes catch on fast and move upwind, looking for clueless trees that haven't gotten the message yet.

That's right: **trees can warn each other** when danger's near. No phones, no emails—just **scent-based** gossip on the breeze.

AIR PLANTS THAT DON'T NEED SOIL

Most plants grow in soil, but air plants (like Tillandsia) don't need it at all. They absorb water and nutrients directly from the air through their leaves.

They often grow on tree bark or rocks, and they thrive in bathrooms, kitchens, and even hanging in the open air.

They're the free spirits of the plant world, no dirt required. And they're perfect for tiny pots or hanging glass globes. Low effort, high cool factor.

THE TREE THAT GROWS UPSIDE DOWN

In dry parts of Africa, there's a strange-looking plant called the **baobab tree**. At first glance, it looks like someone planted it **upside down**: its thick trunk stands tall, but its branches twist and stretch like roots reaching into the sky.

Baobabs store **thousands of liters of water** inside their trunks, which helps them survive in deserts. Some have lived for over **1,000 years,** silently soaking up rain and feeding nearby animals with their giant fruit pods.

Upside down or not, it's one of nature's weirdest (and most useful) trees.

A FLOWER THAT HEATS ITSELF UP

Some flowers don't wait for the sun to warm them—they make their own heat!

The **Eastern skunk cabbage**, found in chilly wetlands, can raise its internal temperature by as much as 60°F (15°C). This helps it melt snow and bloom early in spring, even while the ground is still frozen.

It's like a botanical space heater! Scientists think it uses special cells that "burn" food quickly, like an internal furnace. Bonus: the heat also helps spread its smell... which, as the name suggests, isn't exactly a rose.

THE SPIRALING SUNFLOWER MATH GENIUS

Sunflowers aren't just pretty—they're math geniuses. Their seeds grow in perfect spirals based on a pattern called the Fibonacci sequence.

This natural design helps them pack in the most seeds with the least space. Some pinecones, cacti, and even galaxies use this pattern too!

Nature + math = sunflower power.

QUIZ:
PLANT IT OR NOT?

1) Which plant traps and digests insects?

A) Air plant

B) Venus flytrap

C) Corpse flower

2) What strange smell does the corpse flower produce?

A) Rotten meat

B) Cotton candy

C) Lemon

3) Which plant can launch seeds at over 100 mph?

A) Squirting cucumber

B) Air plant

C) Pando

4) What is special about Pando the tree?

A) It grows upside down

B) It changes colors hourly

C) It's one giant living clone

5) How long did the oldest known lotus seed take before sprouting?

A) 50 years

B) 1,000 years

C) 5,000 years

Answers: 1-B, 2-A, 3-A, 4-C, 5-B

🍀 TRY THIS! 🍀
GROW A PET PLANT

Find a fun plant to grow at home. Try something like bean sprout in a clear jar or an avocado seed in a cup.

Track its growth for 2 weeks. Make a plant diary with:

- Daily drawings or photos
- Any changes you see
- Your guess about what it might do next

Bonus: Give your plant a name and write a short "plant bio" for it!

🌱 BONUS CHALLENGE 🌱
MIX & MATCH PLANT MASHUP

Combine two real plants from this chapter to invent a new hybrid species!

Create a fun profile that includes:

- A name for your plant mashup (e.g., Flytrapaspen or Cucumimosa)
- Its strange combined abilities
- Where it grows
- What makes it special or bizarre

Draw a sketch or describe what it looks like. Bonus points for creativity and weirdness!

CHAPTER 7: DEEP SEA MYSTERIES — WHAT LURKS BELOW?

The deep sea is Earth's biggest mystery zone. It's dark, freezing cold, and full of creatures that look like they swam out of an alien movie. No sunlight ever reaches these depths, but life still thrives, in the most bizarre ways imaginable.

Scientists believe we've explored **less than 10% of** the deep ocean. That means more than 90% of this underwater world is still waiting to be discovered. From glowing predators to pressure-proof beasts, the deep sea is packed with strange surprises.

——————————— 🐙🐙🐙 ———————————

THE DEEP SEA THAT'S BOILING HOT

The bottom of the ocean isn't just cold and dark: some spots are boiling hot.

Near volcanic ridges, **hydrothermal** vents spew out superheated water loaded with minerals. These underwater chimneys can reach 750°F (400°C)—hot enough to melt lead!

Amazingly, entire ecosystems of worms, clams, and bacteria thrive around these vents, living off chemicals instead of sunlight. It's like an alien world... but right here on Earth.

——————————— 🐙🐙🐙 ———————————

THE OCEAN'S GLOWING DISCO PARTY

Some parts of the ocean light up at night, glowing blue-green like underwater fairy dust. This eerie sparkle is caused by **bioluminescence**: a natural chemical glow made by tiny plankton and sea creatures.

When disturbed by waves, boats, or even swimming animals, the water can flash and shimmer. In rare places like the Maldives or Puerto Rico's Mosquito Bay, the glowing effect is so strong it looks like liquid starlight.

It's not magic—it's micro-lights from microscopic life.

——————————— 🐙🐙🐙 ———————————

THE CREATURE THAT TURNS INSIDE OUT

It might sound like a weird defense strategy, but for the sea cucumber, tossing out its own insides is a matter of survival. When attacked, several species eject sticky, stringy guts (some even toxic) to scare off predators.

Don't worry, it can regrow everything in just a few weeks! It's like hitting a panic button and launching spaghetti as a defense.

———————————— 🐌 🐌 🐌 ————————————

THE JELLYFISH THAT MIGHT LIVE FOREVER

The **immortal jellyfish** (Turritopsis dohrnii) may have cracked the secret to eternal life. It can revert its cells to a younger stage and start life over again.

When injured or sick, it turns back into a polyp (the jellyfish version of a baby) and begins the cycle anew. It's not truly immortal (predators and disease still exist), but its ability to reverse aging is unmatched in the animal kingdom.

Move over, superheroes: this jelly is the real deal. It doesn't fear aging—it presses rewind on its life whenever things go wrong.

———————————— 🐌 🐌 🐌 ————————————

THE VAMPIRE SQUID

Despite its name, the **vampire squid** doesn't suck blood. But it does live in the oxygen-poor twilight zone, and it's got style.

It has deep red skin, webbed arms, and glowing photophores that can flash or go dark in a heartbeat. When threatened, it turns itself inside out, flipping its arms over its body and revealing terrifying spines that aren't really sharp—but sure look it.

More Dracula drama than actual danger, but it definitely deserves its spooky name.

———————————— 🐌 🐌 🐌 ————————————

THE GHOST SHARK WITH A WEIRD HEAD

The **chimaera**, also called a ghost shark, lives in the deep ocean and looks like it escaped from a science-fiction movie.

It has a long, rabbit-like face, glowing green eyes, and a venomous spine near its dorsal fin. Some species even have "claspers" on their heads: strange extra appendages used during mating.

It's related to sharks but has a skeleton made of cartilage, not bone—giving it a ghostly glide through the dark waters.

THE FISH WITH A TRANSPARENT HEAD

Meet the **barreleye fish**: a deep-sea wonder with a completely see-through forehead. You can literally see its eyeballs and brain inside its head!

Its eyes are inside a clear, jelly-like dome and can rotate upward to spot prey above or forward to see where it's going. It drifts silently in total darkness, barely moving while tracking tiny animals glowing in the deep.

No one believed it existed until one was filmed by a robotic submarine in 2004. Now it's a fan favorite of deep-sea explorers everywhere.

THE SHRIMP THAT SHOOTS A SONIC BOOM

The **pistol shrimp** may be small, but it's packing a serious weapon: a claw that snaps shut so fast, it creates a bubble bullet that travels at 60 mph.

That bubble collapses with a shockwave louder than a gunshot: strong enough to stun or kill nearby prey. It also creates a tiny flash of light due to the heat from the collapsing bubble.

It's like an underwater laser blaster hidden in a shrimp's claw. Who knew lunch could be so explosive?

THE ANGLERFISH'S GLOWING LURE

The **female anglerfish** is the stuff of nightmares, and genius. She has a glowing rod-like lure dangling from her head, used to attract prey in pitch-black water.

She produces light using **bioluminescent bacteria** that live in the lure. Unsuspecting fish swim toward the glow, only to find themselves dinner.

Males? They're much smaller and often fuse into the female's body for life, becoming little more than a permanent sperm bank. Creepy, but effective!

THE BLOB THAT CAN TURN INTO ALMOST ANY SHAPE

Meet the giant deep-sea octopus, also known as the **dumbo octopus** (named after its flappy ear-like fins).

But here's what's really cool: it has no bones at all, which means it can squeeze through the tiniest cracks, puff up like a parachute, or flatten itself to blend with the ocean floor.

Some deep-sea octopuses can also change color and texture: a shapeshifting strategy that's part escape plan, part camouflage, and all alien-level awesome.

———————————— 🐙 🐙 🐙 ————————————

THE FISH THAT GULPS PREY ITS OWN SIZE

The **black swallower** is a fish with a stretchy stomach that allows it to gulp down prey up to 10 times its size!

Scientists have found specimens with fish still visibly bulging from their bellies. Sometimes, they eat such big meals that they decompose before digestion, causing the swallower to die from its own feast.

That's what you call biting off more than you can chew, literally.

———————————— 🐙 🐙 🐙 ————————————

THE ISOPOD THAT LOOKS LIKE A GIANT PILL BUG

Imagine a roly-poly bug the size of a football. That's the **giant isopod**, a distant cousin of land-dwelling pill bugs. It lives thousands of meters deep and scavenges whatever it can find.

With its armor-plated body and serious frown, it looks like a bug built for battle. It can go **for years without eating**, waiting for a whale fall or sunken fish to appear. When it does feast, it gorges like a deep-sea vacuum cleaner.

Survival here means being patient and extremely tough.

———————————— 🐙 🐙 🐙 ————————————

THE CREATURE THAT THRIVES IN TOXIC VENTS

At the bottom of the sea, vents spew boiling-hot water filled with toxic chemicals. And yet, life flourishes here.

One of the stars of these ecosystems is the **giant tube worm**, which can grow over 8 feet long. It doesn't have a mouth or stomach: it survives thanks to bacteria living inside its body that turn chemicals into food.

This process, called **chemosynthesis**, is like photosynthesis without sunlight. It's life powered by poison gas.

THE DEEP SEA DRAGONFISH WITH INVISIBLE TEETH

The **dragonfish** is a fierce predator with a trick up its jaw: it has transparent, nearly invisible teeth that don't reflect light.

That means prey swimming by in total darkness never sees the attack coming. The teeth are made of a special crystal structure that minimizes reflection.

It also has a "barbel" chin lure and photophores for stealthy hunting. Deep-sea design at its scariest.

🦀 🦀 🦀

THE FISH THAT "WALKS" ON THE OCEAN FLOOR

The **handfish** doesn't swim like a normal fish—it walks.

With fins that look like stubby hands, it strolls along the seafloor in slow, clumsy steps, like a creature from another planet. Found mostly around Australia, it's rare, weird-looking, and rarely moves faster than a crawl.

Its odd little waddle might not win races, but it's proof that evolution takes wild turns in the deep sea.

🦀 🦀 🦀

THE DEEPEST LIVING FISH EVER FOUND

In 2022, scientists discovered a new record-breaker: a **snailfish** swimming nearly 27,000 feet (8,300 meters) deep in the Pacific Ocean, deeper than Mount Everest is tall!

At that crushing depth, the pressure is over 800 times greater than on the surface. Yet this pale, squishy fish thrives in total darkness, surrounded by freezing cold and intense pressure. It doesn't even have scales, just a jiggly body built for the deep.

It's officially the **deepest living fish ever filmed**, a champion of the ocean's "impossible zone."

QUIZ:
HOW DEEP CAN YOU DIVE?

1) Which sea creature has a completely see-through head?

A) Anglerfish

B) Barreleye fish

C) Dragonfish

2) What makes the pistol shrimp dangerous?

A) Its sting

B) Its sonic snap

C) Its venomous tail

3) Which animal can "reset" its life cycle?

A) Immortal jellyfish

B) Handfish

C) Octopus

4) What does the vampire squid do when threatened?

A) Turns invisible

B) Shoots ink

C) Turns itself inside out

5) What helps giant tube worms survive near toxic vents?

A) They eat bacteria

B) They filter chemicals

C) Bacteria live inside them and make food

Answers: 1-B, 2-B, 3-A, 4-C, 5-C

🐙TRY THIS!🐙
CREATE A CREATURE FROM THE ABYSS

Design your own deep-sea creature! Start by asking:

- What depths does it live at?
- How does it see, eat, or defend itself in the dark?
- Does it glow, shoot bubbles, or have giant jaws?

Draw your creature and give it a name, a size, and one terrifying superpower. Bonus points if it has a weird survival trick.

🐚BONUS CHALLENGE🐚
BUILD A DEEP SEA EXPLORER

You're designing a high-tech submersible to explore the deepest parts of the ocean.

Draw or model it and decide:

- How does it handle extreme pressure?
- What tools or cameras does it have?
- What weird creature is it built to discover?

Then write a short *"mission log"* describing the strange new species you just found!

CHAPTER 8: ANIMAL RECORD-BREAKERS – SUPERSTARS OF THE WILD

The animal kingdom is full of champions. From skydiving frogs to lightning-fast falcons, some creatures are so extreme they seem like superheroes! But these wild wonders don't need capes or trophies—they break records just by being themselves.

In this chapter, we'll meet animals that are the **fastest, biggest, loudest**, and **weirdest** at what they do. Whether it's flying faster than a race car or glowing brighter than a lightbulb, these creatures are the **ultimate record-holders** of the natural world.

———————————— 🐒 🐒 🐒 ————————————

FASTEST ANIMAL ON EARTH

If speed had feathers, it would look like a **peregrine falcon**. This sleek bird can dive through the air at over 240 miles per hour—faster than a Formula 1 race car!

Its pointed wings and sharp eyesight make it a master of aerial hunting. When it spots a pigeon or duck from way up high, it tucks into a dive called a "stoop" and rockets toward its target like a feathery missile.

It doesn't just win the gold medal for speed: it shatters the stopwatch.

———————————— 🐒 🐒 🐒 ————————————

STRONGEST ANIMAL (FOR ITS SIZE)

Imagine pulling 1,000 times your own weight. That's exactly what a **dung beetle** does: while rolling balls of poop across the ground.

Not exactly glamorous, but this insect is the ultimate powerlifter. Scientists once watched a male beetle pull the equivalent of a person dragging six double-decker buses!

These beetles aren't showing off: they're building nests and attracting mates. Talk about dirty work.

———————————— 🐒 🐒 🐒 ————————————

LOUDEST LAND ANIMAL

The howler monkey of Central and South America can be heard up to 3 miles away through dense jungle. Males use booming roars to claim territory and warn rivals.

Their large throat sacs act like built-in amplifiers, making them one of the loudest land animals on the planet. Jungle soundtrack? Set to MAX.

— 🐵 🐵 🐵 —

CHAMPION JUMPER

You might swat at them, but **fleas** are actually record-breakers. They can jump over 100 times their own body length, that's like a human leaping the length of a football field!

They don't use muscles alone. Inside their legs is a special protein called *resilin*, which works like a spring-loaded trampoline. When it's released—boing!—they're off like rockets.

For pure jump power, nobody beats the flea.

— 🐵 🐵 🐵 —

BEST NOSE

Sure, you've heard elephants have good trunks, but did you know the **African elephant** has the most powerful sense of smell of any known land animal?

They can smell water from up to 12 miles away and detect the scent of other elephants, humans, and predators with shocking accuracy. Their brain is packed with olfactory receptors: more than any dog or rat ever studied.

If there's a "smell Olympics," elephants take the gold every time.

— 🐵 🐵 🐵 —

FASTEST PUNCH

The **mantis shrimp** may be small, but it packs one of the most powerful punches in the animal kingdom. Its spring-loaded claw can snap forward at 50 mph, creating a shockwave so fast it boils the water and even makes a tiny flash of light!

That's right—its punch can break aquarium glass, crack crab shells, and deliver more force than a bullet (proportionally). Scientists study it for inspiration in building tougher armor and robots.

Basically, it's a shrimp with superpowers.

———————— 🐱 🐱 🐱 ————————

HEAVIEST ANIMAL

Nothing on land or sea comes close to the **blue whale** when it comes to size. At over 180 tons, it's heavier than 30 elephants.

Amazingly, this marine giant feeds on one of the tiniest animals in the ocean: krill. It slurps up mouthfuls of ocean water and filters out millions of shrimp-like snacks.

Biggest creature. Tiniest lunch.

———————— 🐱 🐱 🐱 ————————

HIGHEST-FLYING BIRD

In 1973, a **Rüppell's vulture** collided with a jet flying at 37,000 feet, that's higher than Mount Everest.

These African birds are expert soarers, using hot air currents to cruise for hours while scanning for food. And unlike humans, they don't need oxygen tanks at that altitude.

Nature gave them wings—and lungs to match.

———————— 🐱 🐱 🐱 ————————

MOST VENOMOUS ANIMAL

It's not a cobra, or even a spider. It looks like a floating ghost, but the **box jellyfish** is one of the most dangerous animals on Earth.

Its nearly invisible tentacles can stretch up to 10 feet, and its sting can cause heart failure in minutes. Swimmers barely see it before it's too late.

Even weirder? It has 24 eyes and can actually see shapes—super advanced for a jellyfish!

———————— 🐱 🐱 🐱 ————————

FASTEST SWIMMER

The black marlin is the cheetah of the sea. Clocked at over **80 mph**, it zooms through the ocean like a living torpedo.

Fishermen call it one of the hardest fish to catch: it leaps, it dives, it zips in all directions.

Underwater speed? This fish wrote the book.

———————————— 🐒 🐒 🐒 ————————————

LONGEST SLEEP

Meet the champion napper. The **garden dormouse** can hibernate for more than 11 months straight.

That's longer than some animals are even alive! During hibernation, its heart rate drops and its body barely moves, just enough to stay alive through the cold.

Wake it when spring returns.

———————————— 🐒 🐒 🐒 ————————————

FASTEST LICK

Some salamanders have the fastest tongues on Earth. The **hydromantes** genus, for example, can fire its tongue out to snatch prey in just 7 milliseconds (0.007 seconds), faster than the blink of an eye.

Its tongue is packed like a slingshot in the mouth, then launched with hydraulic-like force. In slow motion, it looks like a rocket-powered sticky dart.

No insect is safe from this forest ninja.

———————————— 🐒 🐒 🐒 ————————————

BIGGEST EYES

The elusive **giant squid** has the largest eyes in the animal kingdom: as big as basketballs!

These enormous eyes help it see in the pitch-black depths, especially when hunting or avoiding predators like sperm whales. A giant squid's eye can detect even the faintest flashes of light from other sea creatures over 300 feet away.

It's like having built-in underwater night vision goggles—times ten.

STRONGEST BITE

The **saltwater crocodile** has the strongest bite ever measured: over 3,700 pounds of pressure per square inch.

That's more powerful than a lion, shark, or even a T. Rex, as scientists estimate! It can crush bones, turtle shells, and anything unlucky enough to get caught in its jaws.

It's a real-life prehistoric power-biter, and it's still ruling rivers today.

🐾 🐾 🐾

MOST ACCURATE HUNTER

Forget lions and sharks—**dragonflies** are the most successful hunters in the animal kingdom.

They catch up to 95% of the prey they chase, thanks to lightning-fast reflexes, incredible vision (nearly 360°), and aerial acrobatics that rival fighter jets.

If dragonflies were human-sized, they'd be the most feared predators on the planet.

🐾 🐾 🐾

SMARTEST BIRD

You've probably heard parrots can talk, but the **New Caledonian crow** can use tools, solve puzzles, and plan ahead.

It's one of the only animals besides humans known to craft tools from sticks, bend wires into hooks, and even solve multi-step problems—just to get food.

Some scientists think these crows are as smart as a **7-year-old child**. Not bad for a bird with a beak and no hands.

🧠QUIZ:🧠
WHO'S THE WILDEST OF THEM ALL?

1) What bird holds the record for highest flight?

    A) Peregrine falcon

    B) Rüppell's vulture

    C) Arctic tern

2) Which animal makes the loudest sound?

    A) Lion

    B) Sperm whale

    C) Howler monkey

3) What animal has the fastest punch?

    A) Gorilla

    B) Octopus

    C) Mantis shrimp

4) Which animal is considered the most venomous?

    A) Poison dart frog

    B) King cobra

    C) Box jellyfish

5) What creature has the largest eyes in the animal kingdom?

    A) Ostrich

    B) Giant squid

    C) Blue whale

Answers: 1-B, 2-B, 3-C, 4-C, 5-B

🐘TRY THIS!🐘
ASK THE CHAMPION!

Choose any record-holding animal and pretend you're interviewing it for a nature magazine.

Write:

- 3–5 questions and the animal's funny, braggy, or humble answers
- Include an "Achievement Bio" and a sketch or photo

Example:

Q: How did you become the world's fastest swimmer?

A: My secret? A pointy nose, powerful muscles, and no time for seaweed.

🐒BONUS CHALLENGE🐒
SUPERPOWER MATCH-UP

List 5–8 animal abilities from the chapter (e.g., speed, camouflage, electric shock, hibernation).

Then ask:

- Which of these powers would YOU want?
- What combo of powers would make the ultimate animal superhero?

Name and draw your hybrid animal.

CULTURES AND GEOGRAPHY

CHAPTER 9: CULTURE QUEST – STRANGE TRADITIONS & COOL CUSTOMS

Imagine this: you're invited to dinner, and when you show up, no one talks. Not a word. Total silence. Would you think it's rude? Or respectful?

Now picture another country, where slurping your noodles loudly is considered *good manners*. Or one where people toss tomatoes at each other on purpose once a year. Sounds weird? Maybe. But only because it's not what you're used to.

In this chapter, we're hopping across continents to uncover the most surprising customs, jaw-dropping festivals, and cultural quirks that make our world wonderfully weird.

——————————— 𝍢 𝍢 𝍢 ———————————

NOODLE SLURPING CONTEST (JAPAN)

In Japan, slurping your noodles isn't rude—it's actually polite! People believe that slurping means you're enjoying your food. It also helps cool the noodles and makes them taste better.

Some cities even host **noodle-slurping contests**, where the loudest, fastest eater wins. It's a delicious mix of manners, speed, and noise! So next time you're slurping spaghetti, you might just be showing world-class etiquette.

——————————— 𝍢 𝍢 𝍢 ———————————

THE BABY-TOSSING FESTIVAL (INDIA)

In the town of Solapur, India, something astonishing happens each year: babies are gently dropped from a rooftop, about 30 feet high, onto a cloth held by people below. And no, it's not a prank!

The tradition, which is more than 500 years old, is believed to bring health and good luck to the child. The drop is slow and carefully done, and the baby always lands safely. Still, it's definitely one of the most surprising customs you'll hear about, especially if you're a new parent.

——————————— 𝍢 𝍢 𝍢 ———————————

BOLIVIA'S DANCING SKELETONS – DÍA DE LAS ÑATITAS

Every year after the Day of the Dead, some Bolivians celebrate **Día de las Ñatitas**—the Day of the Skulls.

People decorate real human skulls, dress them with hats and flowers, and offer them cigarettes or snacks. They believe the skulls bring protection and good fortune to their families.

It might sound spooky, but it's a way to honor the past with joy.

———————————— 𝍐 𝍐 𝍐 ————————————

SWITZERLAND'S GIANT COW PARADE

In the Swiss Alps, the end of summer means it's time for the **Alpabfahrt**, or **cow parade**: joyful event where cows return from mountain pastures wearing flower crowns, bells, and elaborate decorations.

Villagers dress in traditional clothes, musicians play, and families gather to celebrate. The cows steal the show, marching proudly through town like four-legged royalty.

It's not just a parade: it's a celebration of nature, farming, and tradition in one of Europe's most scenic places.

———————————— 𝍐 𝍐 𝍐 ————————————

TOMATO TORNADO – LA TOMATINA (SPAIN)

Once a year, in the town of Buñol, Spain, the streets turn red—not with paint, but with tomatoes. Thousands of people gather for La Tomatina, the world's biggest food fight.

The rule? No anger allowed. It's just messy, squishy fun. Over 100 metric tons of tomatoes are thrown during the event, and by the end, the entire town looks like spaghetti sauce exploded. Locals hose everything down after, and everyone goes home with tomato-scented memories.

———————————— 𝍐 𝍐 𝍐 ————————————

LIP PLATES OF THE MURSI TRIBE (ETHIOPIA)

Among the **Mursi people** in southern Ethiopia, some women wear large clay or wooden plates in their lower lips: a tradition that begins in their teenage years.

The practice is a symbol of beauty, identity, and strength. The plates can grow to the size of a small plate! While the custom may look extreme to outsiders, to the Mursi, it's a powerful part of cultural pride and history.

— 鳥 鳥 鳥 —

INDIA'S COLOR EXPLOSION – HOLI FESTIVAL

Every spring, people across India (and beyond) celebrate **Holi**, a festival that turns the streets into a rainbow war zone.

Friends and strangers throw colored powders at each other, dance, and drench everyone with water balloons and squirt guns. It's a celebration of love, forgiveness, and the return of spring.

You can't leave without looking like a walking piece of art!

— 鳥 鳥 鳥 —

CHEESE ROLLING MADNESS (ENGLAND)

Every spring, brave (or slightly bonkers) people gather in **Gloucestershire, England,** to chase a giant wheel of cheese down a super-steep hill.

The event is called **Cooper's Hill Cheese-Rolling**, and the cheese can roll faster than 70 miles per hour! Competitors sprint, tumble, and somersault downhill in pursuit of it. Most don't catch it (some don't even stay on their feet) but they do earn lots of laughs, bruises, and bragging rights.

— 鳥 鳥 鳥 —

FINLAND'S MOBILE PHONE THROWING COMPETITION

In Finland, people take their old cell phones and... **hurl them as far as possible!**

The Mobile Phone Throwing Championship is a real event where contestants compete for distance and style. Some take it seriously; others wear costumes and scream battle cries.

It's the only sport where being bad at texting might help you win.

— 鳥 鳥 鳥 —

DANCING COFFINS (GHANA)

In Ghana, funerals are not always quiet, tearful events. In fact, they're often full of **music, dancing, and even stunts**, especially by the pallbearers, who carry the coffin in elaborate, choreographed routines.

These "dancing coffin" bearers have become famous online, but they're not doing it to be funny. It's a sign of respect, a celebration of life. Some families even design the coffin in fun shapes (like a fish, a plane, or a Coca-Cola bottle) to reflect the person's passions.

— 鳥居 鳥居 鳥居 —

THE WHISTLING ISLAND (GOMERA, CANARY ISLANDS)

On the island of **La Gomera** in Spain's Canary Islands, people don't just speak: they **whistle**. This isn't bird-talk—it's a full language called **Silbo Gomero**, used to send messages across the island's steep valleys.

Whistles can travel farther than shouted words, especially in the mountains. For generations, farmers and shepherds used Silbo to share news, call for help, or just say hello. The language is even taught in schools to keep it alive today!

— 鳥居 鳥居 鳥居 —

JAPAN'S CRYING BABY FESTIVAL

In Japan, some temples hold a tradition called the **Naki Sumo Festival**, where sumo wrestlers try to make babies cry—on purpose!

Why? The Japanese believe a loud baby cry can scare away evil spirits and bring good health. Two babies face off in a ring, and the first one to cry (or cry the loudest) is the winner!

It's noisy, adorable, and super unusual.

— 鳥居 鳥居 鳥居 —

TOE WRESTLING CHAMPIONSHIP (ENGLAND)

Move over arm wrestling; **toe wrestling** is a real thing, and England takes it seriously! Every summer, the **World Toe Wrestling Championship** is held in Derbyshire, where people go toe-to-toe (literally) to become champion.

Competitors lock big toes and try to pin the other person's foot down. It's silly, fun, and strangely intense. There are even official rules, referees, and training routines. Talk about keeping your toes in shape!

— 鳥居 鳥居 鳥居 —

MEXICO'S NIGHT OF THE RADISHES

Every December, the Mexican city of Oaxaca holds **La Noche de los Rábanos— The Night of the Radishes.**

But these aren't snacks: they're radish sculptures, carved into animals, people, buildings, or even entire scenes from folklore. It's part holiday market, part vegetable art gallery.

Yes, it's an actual competition. Yes, the radishes are HUGE. And yes, the whole thing is rooted in tradition.

SOUTH KOREA'S HAENYEO – SEA WOMEN DIVERS

On Jeju Island, South Korea, groups of elderly women called **Haenyeo** dive into icy cold seas (without oxygen tanks) to collect shellfish and seaweed.

Some are over 80 years old and still diving! It's a tradition passed from mother to daughter, and it's both dangerous and beautiful.

They're living legends of strength and endurance.

♫ ♫ ♫

MONKEY BUFFET FESTIVAL (THAILAND)

In the town of Lopburi, Thailand, monkeys are treated like VIP guests, at least once a year. During the **Monkey Buffet Festival,** locals set up massive feasts of fruits, cakes, and even sodas just for the city's monkey population.

Thousands of macaques roam freely through the streets and temple ruins, enjoying the buffet. It's both a celebration of the monkeys' role in local legends and a way to attract tourists, though you might have to share your snacks! Locals believe feeding them brings good luck and honors the monkey god Hanuman.

It's the world's most banana-filled banquet.

♫ ♫ ♫

GIANT OMELET FESTIVAL (FRANCE)

Every year in the town of **Bessières, France,** people gather to cook a giant omelet—and by giant, we mean more than 15,000 eggs! It's called the **Fête de l'Omelette Géante**, and it all happens in a single massive pan in the middle of the town square.

Chefs use long paddles to stir the sizzling eggs, and then everyone gets a slice. The tradition started to celebrate friendship and sharing... and maybe just a love for breakfast!

🧠QUIZ:🧠
HOW WELL DO YOU KNOW
THE WORLD'S WEIRDEST CUSTOMS?

1) In which country do people throw tomatoes at each other during a giant food fight?

A) Mexico

B) Spain

C) Italy

2) What do some women in Ethiopia's Mursi tribe wear in their lower lips?

A) Gold coins

B) Beads

C) Clay or wooden plates

3) Where do monkeys get their own yearly buffet?

A) Japan

B) Thailand

C) India

4) What do people in England roll down a hill for?

A) A pumpkin

B) A cheese wheel

C) A giant pancake

5) Which island has a language made of whistles?

A) Madagascar

B) Hawaii

C) La Gomera

Answers: 1-B, 2-C, 3-B, 4-B, 5-C

⚑TRY THIS!⚑
CULTURE SWAP CHALLENGE

Time to invent your own **weird-but-wonderful custom!**

Here's how it works:

- Pick one thing everyone does in your country (like eating lunch, greeting people, or celebrating birthdays).
- Imagine a totally different way to do it—one that would seem strange, silly, or surprising to others.
- Draw it, write it, or act it out! Give it a name and a "why we do this" explanation.

Example: "The Great Pajama Parade" – Everyone wears pajamas to school once a year to celebrate getting good sleep. Bonus points if your slippers match!

Be creative, be weird, and most of all—have fun!

🏺 BONUS CHALLENGE 🏺
CULTURAL DEBATE CHALLENGE

You've just read about some of the strangest, coolest, and most surprising customs from around the world. Now it's time to ask yourself:

Would YOU do it?

Pick **any 3 customs** from the chapter and think about:

- Would you try it yourself? Why or why not?
- What do you think would be the most fun? The hardest? The weirdest?
- How is that custom similar to or different from something in your own culture?

Write your answers in a short list, make a comic strip, or talk it out with a friend or family member. Try to see the world through someone else's eyes!

"I'd try cheese rolling, but I'd probably roll myself instead. In my country, we run races, but not after cheese!"

Remember: different doesn't mean wrong—it just means interesting.

CHAPTER 10 :FOOD FACTS TO CHEW ON – FROM SPACE SNACKS TO BANANA TRICKS

You might think food is just about staying alive or filling your belly. But around the world (and even off of it) food has done some pretty weird things. It's floated in zero gravity, exploded on grills, been banned, worshipped, launched, and even confused scientists.

From the fruit that can melt your taste buds to the reason why astronauts need tortillas instead of bread, this chapter serves up the strangest, crunchiest, most mind-blowing food facts ever cooked.

Grab a snack (maybe something normal?)—because things are about to get tasty and totally bizarre.

———————————— 🥐🥐🥐 ————————————

YOU EAT BUGS WITHOUT KNOWING IT

Yep—every year, the average person inadvertently eats about 1–2 pounds of insects, mostly in foods like cereal, chocolate, and peanut butter.

It's perfectly safe (and allowed in small amounts). In many cultures, insects are a normal food: full of protein, and way better for the planet than meat!

So if you've eaten cookies, you might've had a little extra crunch.

———————————— 🥐🥐🥐 ————————————

SQUARE WATERMELONS IN JAPAN

西瓜
¥8000

In Japan, some farmers grow square watermelons—on purpose!

They place young melons inside clear plastic boxes so they grow into cube shapes. Why? It's mostly for decoration and easier stacking in small fridges. But here's the twist: they're often not eaten because they're picked before they're ripe.

Yes, they're fruit-shaped furniture!

POPCORN THAT POPS AT OVER 300°F

Popcorn might seem simple, but every fluffy bite starts with science. Each kernel has a little bit of water inside it. When it's heated to **over 300°F (148.9°C)** the water turns to steam and builds up pressure, until the kernel explodes from the inside out.

That tiny blast is what makes it pop! It's not just a snack; it's a **miniature steam bomb** in a shell. And the best part? No two popcorn puffs ever look exactly the same.

WHY BREAD CRUMBS ARE BANNED IN SPACE

Astronauts don't bring sandwich bread to space. Why? Because bread makes crumbs, and in zero gravity, **crumbs** don't fall. They float around like tiny missiles.

If those crumbs get into machines or a crewmember's eyes or lungs, it can cause serious trouble. That's why space food is often soft, sticky, or served in tubes. Astronauts even use tortillas instead of buns, because they don't crumble!

BANANAS ARE RADIOACTIVE

Yep, you read that right. Bananas are naturally radioactive. But don't worry, they won't give you superpowers or glow in the dark.

Bananas contain potassium, and a tiny portion of that is a type called **potassium-40**, which is slightly radioactive. You'd have to eat **millions of bananas at once** to be in danger. Scientists even use "banana units" to explain radiation levels, because they're such a fun (and safe) example.

THE BANANA IS A BERRY... BUT THE STRAWBERRY ISN'T!

In botanical terms, a **banana** is a **berry**. But a **strawberry**? Not even close!

True berries come from one flower with one ovary and have seeds inside: bananas qualify, but strawberries do not. Botanists call the strawberry a "false fruit". It is actually a multiple fruit which consists of many tiny individual fruits embedded in a fleshy receptacle.

Surprisingly, watermelons, tomatoes, avocados and even eggplants are technically berries too.

TOMATOES WERE ONCE FEARED

Today, tomatoes are a pizza topping and salad star. But hundreds of years ago in Europe, people thought tomatoes were **poison**!

Why? Wealthy people ate off pewter plates: soft metal that reacted badly with the acid in tomatoes. The reaction could cause lead poisoning, but people blamed the tomato, not the dishware. It was called the "poison apple" until science cleared things up... and tomato sauce took over the world.

CHEESE CAN BE ILLEGAL

Not all cheese is created equal. Some cheeses are so smelly, so soft, or so alive with bacteria that they've been **banned in certain countries.**

For example, the French cheese **Casu Marzu** is famous for containing live maggots (yep, really). It's considered a delicacy, but also **illegal** in many places due to health laws. Other cheeses have been stopped at borders just because they smell too strong! So yes, some cheeses are dangerous enough to need a passport check.

KETCHUP USED TO BE MEDICINE

In the 1830s, ketchup was sold as a cure for indigestion!

A doctor in Ohio created "tomato pills" using concentrated ketchup and claimed they had medicinal powers. Even though that turned out to be more hype than help, it shows how foods can move in and out of fashion and function.

Now it's on fries... not prescriptions.

MOST EXPENSIVE SPICE

 Gram for gram, **saffron** costs more than silver. Why? It comes from the delicate red threads inside a **crocus flower**—and it takes 75,000 flowers to make just one pound!

Used in luxury dishes from Spain to India, saffron adds color, flavor, and a price tag that could spice up your wallet.

INSTANT NOODLES WERE INVENTED DURING A FOOD CRISIS

In post-war Japan, food was scarce and people needed quick meals that didn't cost much. Enter Momofuku Ando, who invented the world's first instant noodles in 1958.

All he needed was hot water and a few minutes, and—voilà—**ramen** was born. Today, people eat over 100 billion servings of instant noodles every year, from tiny dorm rooms to high-tech noodle restaurants in space-age cups.

WORLD'S OLDEST CHEWING GUM

The oldest piece of chewing gum ever found is over 9,000 years old! It was discovered in Finland and made from **birch bark tar**, used by Stone Age people to clean their teeth or cure infections.

So next time you're chewing bubblegum, remember: humans have been chewing stuff for health since the Stone Age!

YOU CAN HEAR YOUR FOOD (AND IT TASTES BETTER THAT WAY)

Ever noticed how crunchy snacks taste better when you can hear them crunch? Scientists tested it—and it's true!

In one study, people ate chips while wearing headphones. When the crunch sound was turned up, the chips tasted fresher. When the sound was turned down, they tasted stale. It turns out your ears help your tongue decide what's delicious.

HONEY NEVER SPOILS

You could eat honey that's **thousands of years old**: it would still be safe. Archaeologists found pots of honey in ancient Egyptian tombs, and they were perfectly preserved!

Honey's natural chemistry makes it super hard for bacteria to grow. That's why it was used as medicine in some cultures. So if you find an old jar in the back of the cupboard—don't toss it. Just grab a spoon.

BLUE FOOD? NOT NATURAL (ALMOST)

Blue is one of the rarest colors in natural food. There's no true-blue meat, almost no blue veggies (blue corn is a notable exception), and only a few fruits like plums, some sorts of grapes or blueberries, which are really deep purple.

That's why artificial blue candies and sodas stand out: they look cooler than nature ever intended.

🥐🥐🥐

MUSHROOMS THAT GLOW IN THE DARK

Some mushrooms aren't just tasty: they're glow-in-the-dark! Over 80 species of fungi emit natural light, a phenomenon called **bioluminescence**.

In forests at night, some glowing mushrooms light up logs and fallen trees like nature's nightlights. While not all are edible, some glow-in-the-dark mushrooms are actually used in gourmet cooking. Now that's what you call a bright idea in the kitchen!

🥐🥐🥐

FRUIT THAT TASTES LIKE DESSERT—BUT SMELLS LIKE GARBAGE

The **durian**, known as the "king of fruits" in Southeast Asia, is super spiky on the outside, and super stinky inside. It smells like garbage, onions, and gym socks... but many people say it tastes like sweet almond pudding. It's so smelly, it's banned on planes and trains in some countries!

It's the most loved and feared fruit in the world.

🥐🥐🥐

PIZZA DELIVERY... IN SPACE!

In 2001, Pizza Hut became the first company to deliver pizza to outer space! They sent a vacuum-sealed pie to the International Space Station, where a Russian cosmonaut took the first bite.

It wasn't piping hot, but it was out of this world—and yes, they even tested it in zero gravity first!

🧠QUIZ:🧠
HOW WELL DO YOU KNOW YOUR FOOD FACTS?

1) What fruit smells bad to some but tastes like dessert?

A) Mango

B) Durian

C) Papaya

2) What makes popcorn pop?

A) Oil exploding

B) Steam pressure

C) Magic

3) Which sound can change the way food tastes?

A) Music

B) Your name

C) Crunch

4) Why are bananas slightly radioactive?

A) They absorb sunlight

B) They contain potassium-40

C) They were hit by a meteor

5) What was the original reason tomatoes were feared in Europe?

A) Their color

B) A rumor from pirates

C) Lead poisoning from fancy plates

🥦TRY THIS!🥦
INVENT A NEW SNACK

Time to invent the weirdest, wildest snack the world has never tasted! Let your imagination—and your taste buds—run wild.

1. Give it a name. The sillier or scarier, the better!

2. Choose at least 3 unexpected ingredients. Will it include chocolate and pickles? Marshmallows and mustard?

3. Describe what it tastes like—and what sound it makes when you eat it.

BONUS: Design a snack wrapper with a logo, mascot, or warning label.

"Caution: May cause banana hiccups!"

Then share your snack with a friend—or dare them to imagine eating it!

🍳BONUS CHALLENGE🍳
SNACK SHOWDOWN!

You've just been made head judge at the Weird Food World Championship! Choose 4–5 of the wildest foods from this chapter and give them trophies in categories like:

- Most Surprising
- Most Explosive
- Grossest (but safe!)
- Fancy and Expensive
- Most Scientific

Make your own chart or poster, complete with drawings, emojis, or pretend news headlines:

"Banana Wins for Most Radioactive Energy!"

You can also vote with friends or family and hold your own snack award ceremony.

CHAPTER 11: GAME ON! – WILD FACTS ABOUT SPORTS YOU LOVE

Sure, you've seen a basketball swish through the hoop or a soccer ball launched into the net. You've watched athletes sprint, dive, skate, and spike. But behind every well-known sport is a strange backstory, a forgotten rule, or a record so ridiculous it almost sounds made up.

This chapter isn't about obscure games you've never heard of. It's about the surprising, messy, hilarious history of the sports you already know, and the people who made them weirder, wilder, and way more fun than you ever imagined.

So stretch your brain, not just your muscles. Because what happens off the field might just be more unbelievable than what happens on it.

❖ ❖ ❖

THE FIRST SOCCER BALLS WERE MADE FROM PIG BLADDERS

Long before factories made perfect spheres, soccer balls were, well... kind of gross.

In medieval Europe, the earliest soccer balls were made by inflating pig bladders and wrapping them in leather. They didn't bounce evenly, and they often leaked, but that didn't stop people from kicking them around in chaotic street games.

Eventually, rubber bladders replaced animal parts, and we got the shiny, bouncy balls we know today. Score one for progress.

❖ ❖ ❖

BASKETBALL WAS INVENTED WITH A SOCCER BALL AND PEACH BASKETS

In 1891, gym teacher Dr. James Naismith was trying to invent a new indoor game to keep his students active in winter. He nailed two **peach baskets** to the gym wall and handed players a soccer ball.

There were no dribbles, no three-pointers, and no backboards—just toss the ball in the basket. Oh, and someone had to climb a ladder to get the ball out every time it scored!

Today's fast-paced slam dunks started with fruit baskets and ladders. Talk about a glow-up.

———————————— ⚫ ⚫ ⚫ ————————————

AMERICAN FOOTBALLS USED TO BE ROUND(ISH)

Today's football has that iconic **pointy shape**, perfect for spirals. But the earliest versions of American football used a ball that was round or oval, more like a rugby ball!

In the early 1900s, the ball was redesigned to be narrower and longer, making it easier to throw. That one change transformed football from a run-and-tackle game into a sport full of epic passing plays.

So yes, football's shape literally changed the game.

———————————— ⚫ ⚫ ⚫ ————————————

THE OLYMPIC MARATHON IS THAT DISTANCE BECAUSE OF A QUEEN

Marathon races were first held in 1896, but the distance was not standardized until 1921. The story goes that during the 1908 London Olympics, the British royal family requested the race start at Windsor Castle and finish in front of their viewing box.

That made the course exactly 26.2 miles (=42.195 km), and the distance stuck forever!

———————————— ⚫ ⚫ ⚫ ————————————

THE LONGEST TENNIS MATCH LASTED 11 HOURS AND 5 MINUTES

At Wimbledon 2010, American John Isner and Frenchman Nicolas Mahut played a tennis match that went on... and on... and on.

It lasted over three days, with the final set alone taking 8 hours and 11 minutes. The score? Isner finally won 70–68. Both players were exhausted—and heroes.

After that, tennis rules were changed to prevent matches from going on forever. But the record stands as one of the sport's greatest endurance feats.

———————————— ⚫ ⚫ ⚫ ————————————

ICE HOCKEY ONCE HAD A GAME WITH 92 PENALTIES

Hockey is known for being fast and rough, but one 2004 game between two NHL teams took it to a whole new level.

In a matchup between the Ottawa Senators and the Philadelphia Flyers, tensions boiled over into five massive brawls—in the third period alone. By the end of the game, referees handed out 419 penalty minutes, including 92 separate penalties!

It was one of the wildest games in hockey history: proof that sometimes, the ice gets seriously heated.

———————— ● ● ● ————————

VOLLEYBALL WAS ORIGINALLY CALLED "MINTONETTE"

When **William G. Morgan** invented volleyball in 1895, he was aiming for a less intense version of basketball. He called it "mintonette": a mix of badminton and net play.

The name didn't last, but the idea sure did. Once people realized how much fun it was to volley the ball back and forth over the net, "volleyball" stuck.

Today, it's one of the most played sports in the world, from beaches to Olympic stadiums.

———————— ● ● ● ————————

SUMO WRESTLERS HAVE A SACRED DIET

Sumo wrestlers eat a special dish called chanko-nabe, a protein-packed stew with meat, tofu, and vegetables. They eat enormous portions twice a day: sometimes over 10,000 calories total!

But they don't eat breakfast. Why? Because they train hard first, then eat and nap to gain weight fast. It's a strict tradition, and it's part of becoming a sumo champion.

———————— ● ● ● ————————

HOCKEY GOALIES USED TO FACE FLYING PUCKS WITH BARE FACES

Can you imagine standing in front of a 100 mph slapshot with nothing on your face but a brave expression?

That's what hockey goalies did until the 1950s. The first goalie to wear a **protective mask** was **Jacques Plante**, who had been hit in the face one too many times. At first, people thought it was weak, but soon everyone realized: smart beats stitches.

Now goalie masks are not just safe—they're works of art, each one painted to match the goalie's personality.

———————————— ● ● ● ————————————

RUGBY PLAYERS DON'T WEAR PADS, BUT THEY HIT JUST AS HARD

Unlike American football players, rugby athletes wear almost no padding, but they still tackle, block, and hit just as hard.

How do they avoid getting hurt all the time? Technique! Rugby teaches players to tackle with better form, spreading the impact across the body and avoiding dangerous head hits.

Plus, rugby referees don't mess around. Bad hits get you kicked out quickly, so players learn to be tough and smart.

———————————— ● ● ● ————————————

FIGURE SKATING WAS ONCE ONLY FOR MEN

Believe it or not, figure skating competitions once allowed only men to enter. In the 1800s, women were told it wasn't "proper" for them to skate in public.

That changed in 1902, when **Madge Syers**, a young British woman, entered a men's championship—and placed second! After that, skating opened up to everyone, and today, women's figure skating is one of the most popular Olympic events.

Thanks, Madge, for rewriting the rules—on ice!

———————————— ● ● ● ————————————

JOCKEYS IN HORSE RACING MUST BE TINY, BUT SUPER STRONG

Professional jockeys are usually under 120 pounds, but they need incredible strength and balance to control a galloping horse.

They crouch the entire race, use only their legs to absorb impact, and steer animals weighing over 1,000 pounds, at speeds over 40 mph. Being small helps, but being tough, smart, and fearless is what wins races.

———————————— ● ● ● ————————————

THE HIGH JUMP RECORD THAT HASN'T BEEN BROKEN IN OVER 30 YEARS

In 1993, Cuban athlete Javier Sotomayor jumped an unbelievable 2.45 meters (8 feet and ¼ inch) in the high jump—and *no one has broken his record since.*

That's higher than most ceilings and taller than a giraffe's shoulder! Athletes have come close, but three decades later, Sotomayor's leap still stands tall. It's one of the longest-lasting records in all of sports—and one of the hardest to beat.

—————————————— ● ● ● ——————————————

BASEBALL UMPIRES USED TO STAND BEHIND THE BATTER

In the early days of baseball, umpires didn't stand behind the catcher—they stood behind the batter!

This meant they had to dodge swinging bats while calling balls and strikes. It wasn't until players got faster and more dangerous that the umpire switched to safer ground.

Because nobody wants to get clocked by a bat.

—————————————— ● ● ● ——————————————

QUIDDITCH IS REAL

Inspired by the Harry Potter books, real-life Quidditch is now played at universities around the world. Players run with broomsticks between their legs and follow special rules that mimic the books, minus the flying!

It's now called "**Quadball**" in many places and has its own world championships.

Turns out magic + sports = surprisingly fun.

—————————————— ● ● ● ——————————————

GOLF BALLS HAVE DIMPLES FOR A SUPER WEIRD REASON

Ever wonder why golf balls are covered in **dimples**? It's not just for style.

Those tiny dents help the ball fly farther and straighter. In fact, a smooth golf ball would only travel about half the distance. The dimples reduce air drag and add lift, turning a small white ball into an aerodynamic rocket.

So the next time you slice it into the trees, at least know the ball was doing its best.

🧠 QUIZ: 🧠
ARE YOU A SPORTS SLEUTH?

1) What did players use as a basketball hoop in the earliest games?

   A) Laundry baskets

   B) Peach baskets

   C) Buckets of water

2) What caused the longest tennis match in history to last three days?

   A) Rain delays

   B) No tiebreak rule

   C) A broken scoreboard

3) Why do golf balls have dimples?

   A) To make them bounce higher

   B) To look cool

   C) To fly farther and straighter

4) What was volleyball originally called?

   A) Bounceball

   B) Mintonette

   C) Softnet

5) What were early soccer balls made from?

   A) Animal bladders

   B) Coconuts

   C) Clay and twine

Answers: 1-B, 2-B, 3-C, 4-B, 5-A

🏅 TRY THIS! 🏅
THE MINI OLYMPICS

Ready to move? Time to create your own Mini Olympics with familiar sports, but extra weird rules!

Build 3 game stations using stuff around the house or classroom:

1. **Basketball Bouncer** – Toss a rolled-up sock into a laundry basket, while bouncing on one foot
2. **Slipper Skating** – Slide across the floor in socks or slippers—farthest glide wins
3. **Blindfold Golf** – Try to hit a target using a spoon and ping-pong ball... blindfolded!

Time each round or keep silly scores. Announce the event like a sports commentator!

Short on time? Just try one of the events and challenge a friend!

🏺 BONUS CHALLENGE 🏺
SPORTS SWAP!

Ever wondered what would happen if you mixed tennis with rugby? Or soccer with golf?

In this challenge, you'll invent your own mash-up sport by combining two real ones. The weirder the mix, the better! Here's how:

1. Pick two familiar sports (like basketball and volleyball)
2. Combine their rules, gear, or goals *"You can only score by bumping the basketball over a net!"*
3. Give your new sport a name (like "Volleyballket" or "Rugbasketten")
4. Draw the field or describe the uniform

Add a wild rule—"You must spin before every shot" or "You lose a point if you stop smiling." Get ready to confuse the world... and laugh doing it!

CHAPTER 12:
EXTREME HOMES AND HABITATS
– HOW PEOPLE LIVE IN THE
WORLD'S WILDEST PLACES

Not all homes have front doors, lawns, or rooftops. Around the world, people live in some of the most extreme and surprising places—from deserts so dry it hasn't rained in years to floating villages that rise and fall with the tides.

Some homes are made of ice, others are carved into mountains, and a few are even underground. These are real homes in real places, where kids eat breakfast, do homework, and play, just like you. The only difference? Their homes might sit on stilts, ice, or sand!

Let's tour the world's wildest places to live.

— 🏠🏠🏠 —

THE FLOATING VILLAGES OF CAMBODIA

On Cambodia's Tonlé Sap Lake, entire villages float on water. Houses, schools, stores (even basketball courts) rest on barrels or pontoons. During the rainy season, the lake expands massively, and the homes rise right along with it. In the dry season, the lake shrinks, and the homes float closer together.

Families get around using small boats instead of cars. Kids learn to paddle almost as soon as they can walk! Fishing is a huge part of daily life, and even chores happen from boats: imagine doing your homework while bobbing on the water.

These floating communities are adapted to a landscape that never stands still.

— 🏠🏠🏠 —

THE ISLAND WITH A SINGLE TREE AND A WHOLE TOWN

Tristan da Cunha is the world's most remote inhabited island, sitting in the South Atlantic Ocean, over 1,700 miles from the nearest continent.

Only a few hundred people live there, and there's just one road, one store, and one internet line. Supplies come by boat every few months.

It's a town in the middle of nowhere—and they love it.

LIVING ON A VOLCANO – MOUNT MERAPI, INDONESIA

Mount Merapi is one of Indonesia's most active volcanoes. And yet, thousands of people live on its slopes. Why? The soil is incredibly **rich and fertile,** perfect for growing crops like rice and vegetables.

Volcanic eruptions are dangerous, but residents stay because the land provides everything they need. Homes are built from local stone and wood, and evacuation drills are a regular part of life.

It's risky, but to the people of Merapi, it's also home.

THE UNDERGROUND HOMES OF COOBER PEDY, AUSTRALIA

Welcome to the desert town of **Coober Pedy**, where the sun blazes so fiercely that nearly half the town lives underground. These "dugouts" are carved into hills of soft sandstone. Above ground, temperatures can reach 113°F (45°C), but underground it stays around 73°F (23°C): naturally cool and comfy.

The town started as an opal mining site, and miners discovered they could live inside the hills they were digging. Now, there are underground shops, churches, and even hotels. Rooms are dark, quiet, and free from weather extremes.

It's the perfect place for people who like peace, quiet, and no need for air conditioning.

THE ROCK-HEWN VILLAGES OF IRAN

In Kandovan, a village in northern Iran, homes are carved directly into **cone-shaped volcanic rock formations.** These tall rock towers were formed by lava long ago, and people carved windows, doors, and stairways right into them.

Families have lived here for over 700 years, and many homes have electricity, plumbing, and internet: modern comfort inside ancient stone. The thick rock walls act as natural insulation, keeping homes cool in summer and warm in winter.

Walking through Kandovan feels like stepping into a fantasy world or a real-life hobbit village.

OYMYAKON, RUSSIA – THE COLDEST TOWN ON EARTH

Bundle up! Oymyakon in Siberia is the **coldest permanently inhabited place** on the planet. In winter, temperatures can drop below -76°F (-60°C). The ground is frozen all year round (this is called permafrost) and pipes and vehicles must be specially built to survive it.

Cars must be kept running or they'll freeze solid. People wear multiple layers of fur-lined clothing, and faces are wrapped with scarves to prevent frostbite. Kids still go to school unless the temperature dips below -67°F (-55°C).

Farming is impossible here, so food must be flown in or preserved. Yet people have lived here for generations, showing just how tough humans can be.

ICE HOTELS AND IGLOOS OF THE ARCTIC

In the Arctic and parts of northern Canada, traditional **igloos** were once used by Inuit hunters as temporary winter shelters. These dome-shaped homes were made entirely of snow blocks, cleverly stacked in spirals to form a self-support-ing structure.

Snow might seem cold, but it actually **traps heat inside**, especially when warmed by body heat or a small oil lamp. Modern versions (ice hotels) take it further, with beds, sculptures, and even dining rooms all carved from frozen water.

Guests sleep in thermal sleeping bags and drink from glasses made of ice. It's cold comfort, literally.

THE TREEHOUSES OF PAPUA NEW GUINEA

Deep in the forests of Papua New Guinea, some communities build their homes over **100 feet in the air!** These treehouses are made from wood, vines, and palm leaves and are perched on the tallest trees around.

Why so high? To avoid floods, snakes, wild pigs, and (centuries ago) rival tribes. Today, treehouse living is still practiced in some regions, especially where tradi-tions remain strong.

Climbing a carved tree-trunk ladder is part of daily life. Imagine having a sleepover in the clouds.

ANTARCTICA HAS TOWNS (SORT OF!)

People really do live in Antarctica, just not for-ever.

Scientists and their families stay in special research stations like **McMurdo Station,** where temperatures can drop below -100°F (-73.3°C). There are gyms, greenhouses, and even a coffee shop... but supplies have to be flown in or shipped over ice.

It's one of the coldest, loneliest, and most amazing "neighborhoods" on Earth.

🏠🏠🏠

DESERT TENTS IN THE SAHARA

The **Tuareg** people of the Sahara Desert live in mobile tents made from wo-ven goat hair. These tents are designed to block the sun while allowing cooling breezes to pass through.

As nomads, Tuareg families move to find water and grass for their camels and goats. Kids help pack up tents, load camels, and set up camp in new spots.

Living in the world's largest desert takes skill, strength, and a deep knowledge of the land.

🏠🏠🏠

THE CLIFFTOP VILLAGE OF BONIFACIO, CORSICA

Bonifacio is a historic town perched on **limestone cliffs** overlooking the sea. It's been around for over 1,000 years, with narrow streets, fortress walls, and houses that look like they're about to tumble into the water.

The views are stunning, but living here isn't easy. Strong sea winds, rocky terrain, and limited access make everyday tasks more difficult.

Still, the people of Bonifacio are proud of their cliffside home and its legendary beauty.

THE BAMBOO HOMES OF BALI, INDONESIA

In tropical Bali, many homes are made from bamboo: a fast-growing, sustainable plant that's stronger than it looks. These eco-homes often feature open-air rooms, sweeping spiral staircases, and even bamboo roofs.

They're designed to survive earthquakes, blend with nature, and use minimal electricity. Some even grow food on rooftops or use solar panels.

Living green? These homes take it to the next level.

⌂ ⌂ ⌂

PEOPLE WHO SLEEP IN CAVES—ON PURPOSE!

In **Spain's Granada** region, entire neighborhoods are carved into soft hillsides. These **cave houses** stay **cool in summer and warm in winter**, and many families have lived in them for generations.

They look ordinary from the outside—but step inside, and you'll find modern kitchens, TVs, and cozy bedrooms. It's **underground living with all the comforts.**

⌂ ⌂ ⌂

A DESERT CITY MADE OF MUD THAT'S CENTURIES OLD

The ancient city of **Shibam**, in Yemen, is made almost entirely of mudbrick skyscrapers, some up to 100 feet tall! The city dates back over 500 years and was designed to protect its people from floods and invaders. The tall, narrow buildings were a clever way to save space while keeping cool in the intense heat.

In 1982, it was declared a UNESCO World Heritage Site, recognized for being one of the earliest examples of urban planning using vertical construction.

These buildings have stood for hundreds of years, protected by thick walls and clever air-flow designs. It's often called the "Manhattan of the Desert", and it proves that mud + brains = skyscrapers!

🧠 QUIZ: 🧠
WHERE WOULD YOU LIVE?

1) What town is the coldest inhabited place on Earth?

A) Bonifacio

B) Oymyakon

C) Coober Pedy

2) Why are some homes in Coober Pedy built underground?

A) To hide from animals

B) To stay cool in extreme heat

C) For decoration

3) What do the floating villages of Cambodia rest on?

A) Bricks

B) Rocks

C) Barrels and pontoons

4) Where do people live in homes built into rock towers?

A) Bali

B) Iran

C) Iceland

5) What kind of unusual building material is used in New Mexico earth-ships?

A) Ice

B) Plastic

C) Tires and mud

🏕️ TRY THIS! 🏕️
SURVIVE THAT PLACE!

Could you make it through a day in one of Earth's wildest environments?

Pick one extreme habitat from the chapter—like an ice cave, desert hut, underwater home, or jungle treehouse.

Now look around your home or classroom...

Your challenge:

- Find 3 items that would help you survive in that place (a blanket? a flashlight? a water bottle?).
- Build a mini shelter using pillows, cardboard, or toys—or just describe how you'd stay safe.
- Explain your survival plan: How would you keep warm, cool, or dry? What would you eat or drink?

Present your setup to a friend or family member—would they move in with you?

🧱 BONUS CHALLENGE 🧱
DESIGN YOUR DREAM EXTREME HOME

Time to create the coolest, craziest home ever—in one of the world's wildest places!

Your mission:

- Pick a location (frozen tundra? jungle canopy? deep sea?)
- Describe what your home is made of
- Include one survival feature (like solar water filters or heat-proof walls)
- Add a wild feature—a trampoline floor? Shark-proof windows?
- Name your home like it's a secret hideout or superhero base!

Draw it or build a mini model using LEGO, paper, or recyclables.

HISTORY, INNOVATION AND HUMAN ACHIEVEMENT

CHAPTER 13: KID POWER!
– AMAZING THINGS REAL KIDS HAVE DONE

Think you have to be a grown-up to change the world? Think again. Kids around the globe have done things that scientists, inventors, explorers, and world leaders dream of. Some have made history by inventing new tools. Others have stood up for justice, climbed mountains, or made groundbreaking discoveries: all before finishing middle school!

This chapter celebrates the awesome, inspiring, and totally true stories of young people who did something big. Some of them got famous, and some are just now being recognized. But all of them proved one thing: you don't have to wait to make an impact.

These aren't superheroes from comics. They're real kids, just like you.

—————————— 😊😊😊 ——————————

LOUIS BRAILLE AND THE POWER OF DOTS

When Louis Braille was a child in 1800s France, he lost his eyesight. At age 15, he invented a system of raised dots that allowed blind people to read and write by touch.

Today, his system (**Braille**) is used by millions of people around the world. It opened up education, jobs, and independence for people who had been left out.

One brilliant teenager changed how the world communicates. His invention is so successful that even elevators and bank machines now include Braille numbers.

—————————— 😊😊😊 ——————————

WES LINSTER AND THE DINOSAUR DISCOVERY

Twelve-year-old Wes Linster was hiking with his dad in Montana when he spotted something poking out of a hillside. It looked like a strange rock, but it turned out to be the skull of a horned dinosaur no one had ever seen before!

Scientists later confirmed it was a brand-new species from 75 million years ago. Wes didn't just find a fossil—he helped rewrite the story of Earth's past.

So yes, you really can dig up history on your day off. His find is now preserved in a museum, and Wes got to name the species: a once-in-a-lifetime honor.

———————————— ☺☺☺ ————————————

A TEENAGER CREATED AN APP TO HELP ALZHEIMER'S PATIENTS

At just 12 years old, **Emma Yang** created an app called Timeless to help her grandmother, who was struggling with Alzheimer's disease.

The app uses facial recognition to remind users who people are, when they last saw them, and what their relationships are. Emma learned to code at age 6: by the time she was a teen, she was already using technology to bring comfort and independence to people with memory loss.

———————————— ☺☺☺ ————————————

JACK ANDRAKA AND THE CANCER TEST

At 15, Jack Andraka was devastated by the loss of a family friend to pancreatic cancer. He decided to do something about it. After months of research, he created a simple paper strip that could detect early signs of the disease.

It was faster, cheaper, and more accurate than any existing test. Scientists were stunned.

Jack's invention could save thousands of lives—and it all started with a science project. His work has since earned him awards, scholarships, and the chance to meet global leaders in medicine.

———————————— ☺☺☺ ————————————

ALAINA GASSLER AND THE BLIND SPOT FIX

Most cars have dangerous "blind spots." At 14, Alaina Gassler found a way to fix that. She created a device that uses a projector and camera to show drivers what's hidden by the car's frame.

Her invention won a national science prize and wowed engineers.

Sometimes, solving a big problem starts with one smart idea and a homemade prototype. Alaina built her prototype with the help of garage tools and tested it on her parents' car!

———————————— ☺☺☺ ————————————

MALALA YOUSAFZAI AND HER VOICE FOR GIRLS

Malala began speaking out for girls' education in Pakistan when she was just 11. Even after being attacked for her views, she refused to stay silent.

At age 17, she became the youngest person ever to win the Nobel Peace Prize.

Malala's courage inspired millions. Her message? One voice can change the world. She has since founded a global organization to help girls attend school around the world.

———————— ☺☺☺ ————————

ELIF BILGIN AND THE BANANA PLASTIC

When Elif Bilgin was 16, she learned about how plastic pollution harms animals and ecosystems. She wondered: could plastic be made from something natural instead?

After two years of experiments, she figured it out. She created a **bioplastic made from banana peels**: renewable, biodegradable alternative to petroleum-based plastics. Her invention won international science prizes and caught the attention of global environmental organizations.

Elif's idea showed how innovation and persistence can come from anywhere: including your own kitchen counter.

———————— ☺☺☺ ————————

A 13-YEAR-OLD SOLVED A MAJOR MATH PROBLEM

In 2009, 13-year-old Shouryya Ray from Germany solved a centuries-old physics puzzle first posed by Sir Isaac Newton. It involved calculating how projectiles move through air with resistance—something scientists had struggled to fully explain for over 300 years.

And yes, he solved it for a school project.

———————— ☺☺☺ ————————

THE WORLD'S YOUNGEST AUTHOR WAS FOUR

Dorothy Straight wrote and illustrated a book called How the World Began at age 4 in 1962. Her parents sent it to a publisher just for fun—and it got published by Pantheon Books!

She still holds the record as one of the youngest published authors in history.

———————— ☺☺☺ ————————

A KID INVENTED A DEVICE TO STOP HOT CAR DEATHS

When 10-year-old **Bishop Curry V** heard about a baby who died after being left in a hot car, he decided to do something. He invented a gadget called **Oasis**, which senses heat and movement and sends alerts if a child is left inside a car.

His prototype won awards, and he's working with engineers to bring it to market. One idea, one child—**potentially thousands of lives saved.**

☺ ☺ ☺

GITANJALI RAO AND CLEAN WATER TECH

After hearing about the Flint water crisis, 11-year-old Gitanjali Rao created a device that could test for lead in water more easily than existing tools.

She later developed an app to help prevent cyberbullying and was named TIME Magazine's **Kid of the Year.**

Her motto: use science to help people. Gitanjali continues to teach invention workshops to kids around the world.

☺ ☺ ☺

KATHRYN GRAY AND THE EXPLODING STAR

When 10-year-old Canadian girl Kathryn Gray spotted a tiny bright dot in a telescope image, she wasn't sure what it was. But astronomers confirmed that she had found a **supernova**: a massive star explosion in deep space.

That discovery made her the youngest person ever to spot one. Supernovas help scientists understand the life cycle of stars, and Kathryn's find became part of official space records.

Not bad for a kid who hadn't even finished elementary school. She inspired other kids in her astronomy club to begin hunting for their own discoveries.

☺ ☺ ☺

CAVAN MCCARTHY AND THE ROMAN COINS

In England, 14-year-old Cavan McCarthy was exploring with his metal detector when he found hundreds of Roman coins buried beneath a schoolyard.

His discovery became an official archaeological find and was added to museum collections.

Turns out, recess is a great time for treasure hunting. Cavan's careful documentation of the find helped archaeologists learn more about Roman trade routes in Britain.

———————————— ☺ ☺ ☺ ————————————

A 5TH GRADER DESIGNED A NASA-WINNING SPACESUIT

Alice Liu, a fifth grader from Virginia, won NASA's national competition to design the interior of future **Artemis space missions.**

Her entry included clever storage compartments, compact workout gear, and mental health tools for long trips to the Moon. NASA engineers were so impressed, they incorporated parts of her design into real planning sessions. She helped shape the future of space travel, before finishing elementary school!

———————————— ☺ ☺ ☺ ————————————

BANA AL-ABED AND THE TWEETS FROM A WAR ZONE

At age 7, Bana al-Abed began tweeting from Aleppo, Syria, during a brutal war. She shared what life was like for kids living through bombings and destruction.

Her messages reached world leaders and helped raise awareness about children in conflict zones.

Even in the darkest places, a voice can shine. Bana's tweets became a published book and helped launch her into global advocacy for children in war.

———————————— ☺ ☺ ☺ ————————————

A 6-YEAR-OLD BECAME A MAYOR

Bobby Tufts, a kindergartener from Minnesota, was "elected" as **mayor of the small town** of Dorset—not once, but twice!

Though the town's mayoral race is more symbolic (voted by drawing names from a hat), Bobby took his role seriously: attending parades, visiting the elderly, and promoting kindness. He reminded everyone that even the littlest leaders can make a big impression.

🧠 QUIZ: 🧠
WHAT CAN KIDS DO?

1) Who invented a reading system for the blind when he was a teenager?

A) Jack Andraka

B) Louis Braille

C) Cavan McCarthy

2) What did Kathryn Gray discover in space?

A) A comet

B) A new planet

C) A supernova

3) Who created bioplastic from banana peels?

A) Elif Bilgin

B) Gitanjali Rao

C) Sophie Cruz

4) What did Gitanjali Rao invent to test for?

A) Pesticides in food

B) Lead in water

C) Air pollution

5) Who began tweeting during the Syrian war at age 7?

A) Malala Yousafzai

B) Sophie Cruz

C) Bana al-Abed

Answers: 1-B, 2-C, 3-A, 4-B, 5-C

✍ TRY THIS! ✍
DESIGN YOUR OWN INVENTION

You're a kid inventor. What problem do you want to solve?

Draw or describe your idea:

- What is your invention called?
- What does it do?
- Who does it help?
- What materials would you use?

Get creative—even if your idea sounds wild. That's how real inventions get started. Think about where it would be used, who might need it most, and what makes it different from anything else out there.

💬BONUS CHALLENGE💬
START SOMETHING MINI!

Think of a cause you care about—animals, the environment, kindness, science, anything! Now design a "mini movement" you could start at your school or in your neighborhood.

Plan it out:

- What's your goal?
- Who would join you?
- What would you name your movement?
- What's the first thing you'd do to get it started?

Even big movements start with small steps—and you can take one today.

CHAPTER 14: ART THAT SINGS, MUSIC THAT PAINTS – CREATIVE FACTS THAT ROCK

Think art is just quiet museums and music is only about dancing? Think again.

Around the world, people have painted with beet juice, sculpted in butter, played music made from ice, and even launched songs into space. Some paintings take years to finish, others disappear in a flash. Some songs heal, some hypnotize— and some are so catchy, they've been stuck in people's heads for centuries.

In this chapter, we'll explore the quirkiest, most colorful corners of human creativity. So get ready to tap your toes, squint at strange sculptures, and find out just how weird art and music can really get.

--- 🎨 🎨 🎨 ---

THE PAINTING THAT TOOK 12 YEARS TO FINISH

Leonardo da Vinci's **Mona Lisa** is one of the most famous paintings in the world. But did you know it took him over 12 years to finish it?

Leonardo was a perfectionist. He kept tweaking tiny parts, especially the smile. Even after it was done, he carried it around with him instead of delivering it to the person who commissioned it. Some people say he was obsessed with it. Others say he just couldn't stop improving it.

More than that: Leonardo was a left-handed genius who could write and draw with both hands at the same time! He often wrote in **mirror writing**, flipping letters backward as if seen in a mirror. Some historians think this was to keep his ideas secret, while others believe it was just easier for him. His notebooks are filled with inventions, science, and sketches, all written in his own uniquely brilliant way.

SONGS THAT HAVE BEEN TO SPACE

When astronauts travel off Earth, they don't just take tools—they take tunes.

The first song ever played in space? *Jingle Bells,* performed on a harmonica and sleigh bells during a surprise holiday prank on NASA radio. Since then, crews have brought everything from classical music to classic rock. One astronaut even woke up every morning to David Bowie's Space Oddity.

Some spacecraft even carry golden records with Earth's greatest music: just in case aliens are listening.

A SCULPTURE MADE OF BUTTER

At some state fairs in the U.S., artists don't just carve wood or clay—they carve **butter**.

One of the most famous examples is the life-sized butter cow at the **Iowa State Fair.** It's made entirely from creamy yellow butter and kept cool in a refrigerated display case. Artists use special tools (and very cold hands) to sculpt incredibly detailed shapes. Butter art may melt away, but it sure makes a lasting impression.

ANCIENT THEATERS HAD SPECIAL EFFECTS!

Greek and Roman plays were more than actors in togas—they used mechanical stage tricks like trapdoors, rolling scenery, thunder machines, and even cranes that "flew" actors across the stage to play gods.

This system was called **"Deus ex machina",** or "god from the machine," and it became so common that today it's a term for any sudden, surprise ending in stories.

So yes, ancient art came with pyrotechnics and wire work, just like Hollywood!

THE PAINTING THAT VANISHES WHEN TOUCHED

There's a kind of ink used by modern artists that disappears when heated—even from body heat!

At some museums, people have seen paintings fade or change color when they hover a hand near them. The trick is **thermochromic paint,** which reacts to temperature changes. Some artworks even reveal hidden pictures as they warm up!

THE WORLD'S LARGEST MUSICAL INSTRUMENT

You might think the largest instrument is a giant tuba or enormous drum, but it's actually **a cave.**

Inside Luray Caverns in Virginia, there's the **Great Stalacpipe Organ**, which taps on the cave's stalactites using rubber mallets. The vibrations echo through the entire space. You can hear the whole cave sing—and yes, you can play real songs on it.

SINGING ICE (YES, REALLY)

In frozen places like Norway and Canada, musicians have created real instruments made entirely from ice—and performed full concerts with them!

There are ice drums, ice xylophones, even ice violins. As the musicians play, the instruments slowly melt, making every performance one of a kind. It's called **ice music,** and it's both cool and magical.

ANDY WARHOL MADE SOUP... FAMOUS

In the 1960s, Andy Warhol shocked the art world by painting a can of Campbell's Soup—and calling it art. He didn't stop at one can: he painted 32 different flavors, just like you'd see in a grocery store.

Warhol became the superstar of **Pop Art**, a movement that turned everyday things into bold, colorful artwork. He once said, "I want to be a machine," and even had assistants in his "Factory" help mass-produce his pieces.

From soup cans to celebrities, Warhol proved that anything can be art, if you look at it differently.

A PAINTING MADE OF PANCAKES

Some food artists have turned breakfast into a canvas: **by painting portraits with pancake batter!**

It's not just about flipping circles. Artists use squeeze bottles to control how the batter flows, pouring darker shades first and lighter ones later. Some make cartoon characters, others create realistic faces with wild detail. On hot griddles, the pancakes cook while the art forms—fast!

When it's done, you have a golden, edible masterpiece. And yes, you can eat it... but some are so cool, people take selfies with their pancakes first.

———————— ☺ ☺ ☺ ————————

MOZART WROTE A SONG THAT'S ALL ABOUT FARTING

Yes, that **Mozart**—the musical genius who wrote symphonies and operas—also had a silly side. He once wrote a short piece called "Leck mich im Arsch" (in German), which roughly translates to... well, "Kiss my behind."

Mozart loved wordplay, pranks, and jokes, even in music. It proves that even classical composers sometimes goofed off at the keyboard.

———————— ☺ ☺ ☺ ————————

MUSIC THAT MAKES YOU SHOP SLOWER

Have you ever walked into a store and heard gentle music playing? That's not just for fun.

Studies show that slow music makes people **walk slower and shop longer,** while fast music makes them move quickly. Some stores even use music to make you feel hungry or cozy.

Turns out, the playlist might be controlling your shopping cart!

———————— ☺ ☺ ☺ ————————

A VIOLIN MADE FROM TRASH

In a town in Paraguay, kids formed an orchestra, but had no money for instruments. So, they made their own.

Using old oil cans, metal spoons, and discarded wood, they built working violins, drums, and guitars. Their group, the **Recycled Orchestra,** now tours the world, proving that music can come from anything, even garbage.

———————— ☺ ☺ ☺ ————————

THE MYSTERIOUS SINGING ROAD

In South Korea and a few other places, there are roads that play music when you drive over them!

Special grooves cut into the road make your tires vibrate to create notes. If you drive at just the right speed, you can hear songs like *Mary Had a Little Lamb.* They're called **musical roads,** and they're made to entertain and encourage safe driving.

COLOR MUSIC: SEEING SOUND AND HEARING COLOR

Some people have a condition called **synesthesia**, where senses mix together in amazing ways.

They might see colors when they hear music, or taste shapes when reading words. Famous musicians like Billie Eilish and Duke Ellington said they could "see" sound as colorful patterns.

It's like your brain turns every concert into a light show!

ANTIQUE STATUES USED TO BE PAINTED IN BRIGHT COLORS

You've probably seen ancient Greek and Roman statues—smooth white marble, right? Surprise! **They were never meant to be white.**

Back in the day, these statues were painted in **bold, bright colors**: with red lips, golden armor, and even blue hair! Over thousands of years, the paint wore off, leaving the pale marble we see in museums today.

So next time you see a statue of a Greek god, imagine it **decked out like a superhero!**

THE MYSTERIOUS ARTIST NOBODY CAN CATCH

Imagine being one of the most famous artists in the world... but no one knows who you are. That's the case with **Banksy**, a graffiti artist whose powerful, funny, and mysterious street art has popped up all over the world.

He works in secret, often at night, sneaking into public places to paint murals with political messages or funny surprises—then vanishes without a trace. Some of his artwork has sold for millions (like a framed copy of his "Girl with Balloon", auctioned at Sotheby's in 2018 for £1,042,000), but Banksy himself has never revealed his real name.

He's like the ninja of the art world, painting in the shadows.

🧠 QUIZ: 🧠
ART & MUSIC MIX-UP!

1) What is the Mona Lisa famous for?

A) Being painted with pancake batter

B) Taking 12 years to finish

C) Playing music

2) What happens when you drive over a musical road?

A) It plays a song

B) Your tires get louder

C) You drive faster

3) What is the famous cow statue at the Iowa State Fair made from?

A) White chocolate

B) Soap

C) Butter

4) What's special about the Great Stalacpipe Organ?

A) It's made of candy

B) It plays the cave itself

C) It's a drum kit

5) What's it called when people see colors when they hear music?

A) Colorvision

B) Spectrasound

C) Synesthesia

Answers: 1-B, 2-A, 3-C, 4-B, 5-C

♪♪TRY THIS!♪♪
SYNESTHESIA SOUND LAB

Some people hear music and see colors. Others see shapes when they hear sounds. It's called **synesthesia**, and now you get to try it—whether your brain works that way or not!

Here's your creative mission:

1. Choose a short piece of music—any song or melody.
2. While listening, draw or color whatever comes to mind.
   - What colors do you see in the sounds?
   - Are they soft swirls or sharp lines?
   - Do drums look different from violins?

You can use crayons, markers, watercolor—anything!

BONUS: Make a mini art gallery of "music posters" based on different songs. Give each one a title, like "Bass Boom in Blue" or "Rainbow Trumpet."

No two people will make the same art—and that's the beauty of it.

🖼️BONUS CHALLENGE🖼️
THE GREAT ART DEBATE CHALLENGE

Art doesn't always come in frames. Some of it melts (like butter sculptures), changes color (like heat-reactive paint), or even sings (like caves and roads!).

Now it's your turn to decide what counts as art.

1. Pick 3 things from this chapter (or your own ideas):
   - A pancake painting
   - A violin made of trash
   - A painting that disappears when touched
2. Debate or decide: *Is it art or not? Would you hang it in a gallery? Would you want to make it?*

Try this with a friend or family member—and don't be afraid to disagree. The best part of art is that everyone *sees it differently.*

CHAPTER 15: EPIC BUILDS – STRANGE, TALL, AND TOTALLY AWESOME

Skyscrapers that touch the clouds. Ancient cities carved into cliffs. Bridges built upside down. Humans have been building wild, brilliant, and downright bizarre things for thousands of years—and we're still at it.

Some structures took centuries to complete. Others were slapped together quickly but became world-famous. Some are made of marble, others of salt, bones, bamboo, or even ice. And then there are the buildings that were never supposed to stand up at all, but somehow still do.

In this chapter, we'll climb, tunnel, and tilt our way through some of the most jaw-dropping human-made structures ever imagined. You'll discover the world's weirdest bridges, the tallest towers, and monuments so strange they've become legends.

Let's explore the buildings that prove human imagination isn't just big—it's built to last.

THE LEANING TOWER WHICH WAS NEVER MEANT TO LEAN

Italy's famous **Leaning Tower of Pisa** is one of the most recognized buildings in the world, but its most famous feature was a big mistake.

Construction began in 1173, but the soft, uneven ground beneath the tower made it start tilting almost immediately. Builders tried to fix it by making one side taller than the other, but that only made it worse!

Today, it leans about 4 degrees. Engineers have stabilized it, so it won't fall anytime soon, but it's still the world's most famous architectural accident.

THE GREAT WALL OF CHINA WAS BUILT WITH STICKY RICE

You've heard of the **Great Wall of China**, but did you know that parts of it were built using a secret ingredient from the kitchen?

During the Ming Dynasty, engineers mixed sticky rice porridge with slaked lime to create a kind of ancient super-cement. The result? A mortar so strong it has helped the wall survive earthquakes, floods, and centuries of weather.

Modern scientists tested it and found that this "rice mortar" is tougher than some modern concrete. Now that's what you call a recipe for success.

———————————— ⚉ ⚉ ⚉ ————————————

THE PYRAMID THAT REIGNED AS THE TALLEST FOR AGES

The **Great Pyramid of Giza** in Egypt is one of the most astonishing structures ever built. It was made as a tomb for the pharaoh Khufu, using more than 2 million stone blocks, each as heavy as a small car!

The design is so precise—perfectly aligned with the stars and compass points—that scientists still puzzle over how it was built without machines or modern tools.

For nearly 4,000 years, no building on Earth stood taller. Not bad for something built with hammers, chisels, and genius.

———————————— ⚉ ⚉ ⚉ ————————————

PETRA WAS HIDDEN FOR CENTURIES

Tucked into the red sandstone cliffs of Jordan, the ancient city of **Petra** was carved directly into the rock more than 2,000 years ago. Its most famous building, the Treasury, looks like a palace from a fantasy movie, but it's real.

For centuries, the entire city was forgotten, hidden by desert sands. It wasn't rediscovered by the outside world until 1812! Today, it's one of the most breathtaking archaeological sites on Earth.

Petra shows what happens when humans carve cities instead of building them—and how some structures are too amazing to stay lost forever.

———————————— ⚉ ⚉ ⚉ ————————————

THE TOWER THAT REACHED TOO FAR

According to legend, in ancient Babylon people tried to build a tower so tall it could touch the sky. They started stacking bricks higher and higher, but then—uh-oh—no one could understand each other! Suddenly, people were speaking different languages, and the great project collapsed into confusion.

That tower became known as the **Tower of Babel.** Historians aren't sure if it was real or a story to explain why people speak different languages, but there indeed was a huge religious structure in Babylon called a *ziggurat*, and it was massive.

A TEMPLE CARVED FROM A SINGLE ROCK

In the town of Ellora, India, there's a temple so massive and detailed, you'd think it took a whole city to build it. But it was carved from just one single piece of volcanic rock.

It's called the **Kailasa Temple**, and builders started at the top of the rock and carved downward, removing over 200,000 tons of stone without machines. No glue. No bricks. Just chisels, hammers, and genius.

The scale, symmetry, and beauty of the temple still leave architects scratching their heads. How did they do it? No one knows for sure.

☆ ☆ ☆

A FLOATING GARDEN IN THE DESERT?

Imagine lush green vines, colorful flowers, and waterfalls flowing down stone terraces—all in the middle of a hot, dry desert. That's the idea behind the **Hanging Gardens of Babylon**, one of the ancient world's biggest mysteries. According to ancient writers, this garden wasn't just beautiful—it was built on giant stone platforms, with water pumped up from the river far below.

But here's the mystery: no one's sure it was real. No ruins have ever been found, and some believe the garden was actually in another city, or just a legend.

Still, the idea of a sky garden in the desert is so cool that it's stayed in our imagination for over 2,000 years.

☆ ☆ ☆

A CHURCH THAT'S STILL UNDER CONSTRUCTION... AFTER 140 YEARS

In Barcelona, Spain, the **Sagrada Família** is one of the world's most famous buildings, and it's still not finished.

Construction began in 1882, and it's so detailed, with towers and carvings and colorful glass windows, that builders are still working on it today. The original architect, Antoni Gaudí, died before it was halfway done.

Once completed, it will be the tallest church in the world. But even unfinished, it attracts millions of visitors a year, and proves that good things take time... sometimes a lot of time.

THE DEEPEST INDOOR POOL IS LIKE A SINKHOLE

Want to swim in a building and take a dive 200 feet down? Visit **Deep Dive Dubai**, home to the deepest indoor pool in the world.

It's not just deep, it's built like an **underwater city**, with sunken rooms, fake ruins, and even a bicycle for scuba divers to "ride." The pool is so deep that scuba divers can descend into total darkness—and even train for space missions.

Swim goggles not included... but maybe bring a submarine.

THERE'S A HOTEL MADE ENTIRELY OF ICE

Every winter in Jukkasjärvi, Sweden, a hotel is built from scratch using ice and snow, and when spring arrives, it melts away!

The **ICEHOTEL** includes walls, beds, glasses, even chandeliers made of frozen water from a nearby river. Artists from around the world come each year to sculpt the hotel's icy rooms. Guests sleep in thermal sleeping bags on beds covered in reindeer skins.

It's chilly, magical, and 100% temporary: gone by April, back by December.

THE WORLD'S TALLEST BUILDING MOVES WITH THE WIND

At 828 meters (2,717 feet), **Burj Khalifa** in Dubai is the tallest building on Earth. It's so high that the air at the top is cooler than at the base, and you can watch the sunset twice: once from the ground and again from the top!

But here's the coolest part: it's designed to sway in the wind. Just a little. Without that flexibility, the building might crack under pressure. Its spiral shape also helps it cut through desert gusts like a giant needle.

Yes, the Burj can "wiggle"—and that's what keeps it standing tall.

A SKYSCRAPER WAS BUILT ON ROLLERS TO SURVIVE EARTHQUAKES

In earthquake-prone Japan, engineers created an office building that doesn't resist shaking: it rides it out.

The Shinjuku Mitsui Building in Tokyo was placed on massive steel rollers and rubber pads, allowing it to slide gently during a quake. It's like the building has built-in shock absorbers, just like a car!

This technique, called base isolation, is now used in earthquake zones around the world, and it works so well, people inside may not even feel the tremors.

▲▲▲

THERE'S A BRIDGE THAT'S ALSO A TREE

In the Indian state of Meghalaya, you'll find bridges that weren't built: they were grown.

Locals train the roots of rubber fig trees to stretch across rivers, guiding them over wooden scaffolds. Over time, the roots grow into sturdy, living bridges that can last for hundreds of years and hold dozens of people.

These living root bridges are eco-friendly, self-repairing, and absolutely stunning: a perfect blend of nature and human ingenuity.

🧠 QUIZ: 🧠
BUILD YOUR BRAIN!

1) What unusual ingredient helped hold parts of the Great Wall of China together?

   A) Sand

   B) Clay bricks

   C) Sticky rice

2) What makes the living root bridges of India so special?

   A) They're built by elephants

   B) They're grown from tree roots

   C) They float on water

3) What surprising feature helps the Burj Khalifa stay standing in strong winds?

   A) It's made of rubber

   B) It has fans inside

   C) It sways slightly

4) Where is the hotel made entirely of ice rebuilt every winter?

   A) Canada

   B) Sweden

   C) Norway

5) Why is the Sagrada Família in Spain so famous?

   A) It's the tallest building on Earth

   B) It's shaped like a castle

   C) It's still under construction after over 140 years

🏗️ TRY THIS! 🏗️
DESIGN YOUR DREAM STRUCTURE

If you could build any structure in the world—no rules, no budget, no limits—what would it look like?

Here's your blueprint challenge:

1. Pick a location (on land? undersea? on a cloud?)
2. Decide its purpose: Is it a house, a theme park, a museum, or something totally new?
3. Give it a wild feature—maybe it glows, moves, floats, or changes shape
4. Sketch it and give it a name

Bonus: Label the materials you'd use. (Chocolate bricks? Bamboo scaffolding? Solar panels made of seashells?)

Pro tip: Weird is wonderful in architecture—go big, go bold, go bonkers.

🏙️ BONUS CHALLENGE 🏙️
PITCH IT! ARCHITECTURE SHOWDOWN

You've seen the world's wildest buildings—now it's time to **sell your own!**

In this challenge, pretend you're an architect with a bold idea. Your job? Convince someone that your design deserves to be built.

1. Pick a real or imaginary structure (you can use your "Try This!" design)
2. Prepare a 1-minute pitch. Include:
   - What the building does
   - Why it's exciting, useful, or important
   - What makes it unforgettable
3. Perform your pitch for a friend, teacher, or family member. Use props or sketches if you like!

Bonus twist: Compete with someone else's design. Take turns "pitching" and let your audience vote on the winner.

CHAPTER 16: STRANGE BUT TRUE – REAL HISTORY'S WEIRDEST MOMENTS

When you hear the word 'history', you might picture serious people in old paintings, wearing powdered wigs and talking about battles and laws. But real history? It's way stranger than that.

It's a place where rulers made up their own rules, wars began over everyday objects, and people sometimes danced until they dropped. It's where the unexpected wasn't rare—it was normal. In fact, if you time-traveled back a few hundred years, you might not believe what you were seeing.

In this chapter, we're pulling back the curtain on the most bizarre, hilarious, and head-scratching true events from the past. Some are mysterious. Some are ridiculous. And all of them really happened

$$\partial\,\partial\,\partial$$

THE EMPEROR WHO APPOINTED A HORSE

In ancient Rome, power was everything. But one emperor, **Caligula**, took power to a very strange place. He loved his horse, Incitatus, more than most people. He gave the horse a marble stable, a jeweled collar, and even a house!

But here's where it gets truly strange: Caligula tried to make his horse a **senator**. Some historians think it was a joke, or perhaps a way to insult the real senators. Either way, it's one of the most famous "what was he thinking?" moments in history.

$$\partial\,\partial\,\partial$$

ALLIGATOR IN THE WHITE HOUSE

Most U.S. presidents have had dogs, or maybe a cat or two. But **John Quincy Adams**, the 6th president, had something way stranger: an alligator!

The story goes that the alligator was a gift from a French general and lived for a time in the White House bathroom. President Adams thought it was hilarious and loved watching guests panic when they discovered it. He eventually moved the alligator out, but not before earning a spot in the history books for having the weirdest White House pet of all time.

THE WAR OVER A WOODEN BUCKET

Imagine going to war over... a bucket. In 1325, the Italian cities of **Modena** and **Bologna** had been rivals for years. Then, one day, some Modenese soldiers stole a wooden water bucket from Bologna's town well. That's all it took.

Bologna demanded it back. Modena refused. And just like that, the War of the Bucket began. Thousands of soldiers fought, hundreds died—and yes, Modena kept the bucket. You can still see it today in a museum.

ANCIENT ROMANS CLEANED WITH PEE

Yes, really. The ancient Romans used human urine to bleach their clothes and even clean their teeth. Why? Because urine contains ammonia: a powerful cleaning agent.

They even had public pee pots, and tax collectors charged fees to urine collectors.

It might sound gross, but it was just another day in Rome. When in Rome... bring mouthwash.

A KING DIED FROM EATING TOO MUCH DESSERT

King Adolf Frederick of Sweden died in 1771 from eating himself to death, after consuming an enormous royal feast topped off with 14 servings of semla, a rich Swedish dessert made with cream, pastry, and marzipan.

His death is remembered more for its weirdness than its tragedy. In Sweden, he's sometimes called "the king who ate himself to death."

It's a royal tale that reminds us: even kings should save room for later.

THE TIME THE EIFFEL TOWER WAS ALMOST TORN DOWN

Today, the **Eiffel Tower** is one of the world's most famous landmarks, but did you know it was originally meant to be **temporary**?

Built for the 1889 World's Fair in Paris, it was supposed to stand for just 20 years. Many Parisians hated it and called it ugly. Some wanted it gone!

But when radio antennas were added to the top, it became useful—and survived. Now, it's the symbol of Paris, saved by technology and a twist of fate.

EXPLODING WHALE ON THE BEACH

In 1970, a dead whale washed up on the coast of **Oregon, USA.** Officials weren't sure what to do with the 8-ton stinker... so they filled it with dynamite.

Their plan? Blow it to bits so seagulls could clean up the mess. But when they set off the explosion, giant chunks of whale rained down on cars, buildings, and horrified bystanders.

It was a very real (and very smelly) esson in what **not** to do with a dead whale.

THE DANCING PLAGUE

One summer day in 1518, a woman in Strasbourg (now France) started dancing in the street—and wouldn't stop. Within a week, dozens had joined her. Some danced for days without rest, collapsing from exhaustion.

This wasn't a party: it was a mystery. People danced uncontrollably, some to their deaths. Historians call it the **Dancing Plague**, and it's still unexplained.

Was it mass hysteria? A reaction to poisoned bread? Or something stranger? No one knows why so many people just... couldn't stop moving.

THE GREAT EMU WAR

In 1932, Australia declared war. Not against another country: against emus. These giant, flightless birds were damaging farmland, and the government sent soldiers to deal with them.

Armed with machine guns, the soldiers tried to drive the emus away. But the birds were too fast, too scattered, and too good at hiding.

Final result? Emus: 1. Soldiers: 0.

It's probably the only war in history where humans were **defeated by birds.**

A CALENDAR THAT SKIPPED 11 DAYS

When England changed from the Julian calendar to the Gregorian calendar in 1752, something weird happened: they had to skip 11 days. People went to bed on September 2, and when they woke up, it was September 14.

Some people panicked. "Give us back our 11 days!" they shouted. They thought the government had stolen part of their lives. It took a while, but eventually everyone got used to the new time system, which we still use today.

THE EMPEROR WHO TRIED TO OUTLAW DEATH

In ancient China, **Emperor Qin Shi Huang** wanted to live forever. He searched for potions, built palaces to avoid bad luck—and even banned anyone from mentioning the word "death" in his presence.

Ironically, he may have died from **mercury poisoning**—because he took pills that were supposed to make him immortal.

His enormous tomb remains mostly unexcavated, possibly surrounded by **rivers of liquid mercury.** Talk about weird (and dangerous) history.

A PRESIDENT FOUGHT A DUEL... AND GOT SHOT

In 1806, **Andrew Jackson**, who would later become the 7th U.S. president, fought a duel over an insult to his wife. His opponent fired first and hit Jackson in the chest.

But Jackson didn't flinch, he calmly aimed and shot his opponent dead.

The bullet in Jackson's chest was never removed, and he carried it for the rest of his life. Talk about holding a grudge... and a souvenir.

THE GREAT KETCHUP DEBATE

In the 1800s, ketchup wasn't just a topping for fries—it was sold as **medicine**! A doctor named John Cook Bennett claimed tomato ketchup could cure diarrhea, indigestion, and even jaundice. He even turned it into a pill.

People believed it for a while, until real doctors stepped in and said, "Um... no." Ketchup went back to being a tasty condiment, but for a short time, it had a very weird side job as a superhero snack.

NAPOLEON WAS ATTACKED BY BUNNIES

In 1807, after a military victory, **Napoleon Bonaparte** decided to hold a rabbit hunt to celebrate. His men released hundreds of bunnies into a field, expecting a grand chase.

But the rabbits didn't run away. Instead, they charged toward Napoleon and his officers in a fluffy swarm! Why? The rabbits had been tame farm bunnies, and they thought they were being fed.

Napoleon had to flee in his carriage, chased by a sea of hopping furballs. That day, one of history's greatest generals was defeated by bunnies.

ꙮ ꙮ ꙮ

A PIRATE QUEEN RULED THE CHINESE SEAS

In the early 1800s, a woman named **Zheng Yi Sao** (she also went by several other names) commanded over 70,000 pirates in the South China Sea: more than most navies!

She created her own pirate laws, defeated government fleets, and eventually retired... peacefully, with a full pardon.

She's considered one of the most powerful pirates in history—and she didn't even need a parrot or a peg leg.

ꙮ ꙮ ꙮ

THE TIME THE CIA TRIED TO SPY USING CATS

During the Cold War, the CIA had an odd idea: what if cats could spy on enemies? They created **"Acoustic Kitty,"** a project to surgically implant microphones and antennas into cats.

They released one cat near a Soviet building, but it was hit by a taxi minutes later.

The project was quickly shut down. It turns out, cats are better at chasing mice than keeping secrets.

🧠QUIZ:🧠
HOW WELL DO YOU KNOW HISTORY'S WEIRDEST MOMENTS?

1) What animal did Napoleon get ambushed by?

A) Goats

B) Rabbits

C) Cats

2) What did the War of the Bucket start over?

A) Gold

B) A hat

C) A wooden bucket

3) What made the emus "win" in Australia?

A) They outsmarted the army

B) They flew away

C) They teamed up with kangaroos

4) What happened during the Dancing Plague?

A) People danced for days

B) The town threw a festival

C) Musicians played nonstop

5) What happened to the calendar in 1752?

A) A month disappeared

B) A whole year was skipped

C) 11 days vanished overnight

Answers: 1-B, 2-C, 3-A, 4-A, 5-C

🐋 TRY THIS! 🐋
STRANGE HISTORY CHALLENGE CARDS

Ready to get weird? Create your own set of Strange History Challenge Cards and test your knowledge and your creativity.

How to make them:

1. Cut a few blank pieces of paper into card-sized shapes.
2. On each one, write a silly challenge inspired by a real fact from this chapter.
3. Shuffle them and take turns drawing a card with a friend, parent, or sibling.

Here are some example cards to get you started:

- "Do an emu run" – Waddle across the room as fast as you can without using your arms!
- "Bucket Battle!" – Pretend you're a knight guarding the last wooden bucket on Earth.
- "Horse in the Senate" – Deliver a serious speech about hay laws, like Caligula's horse.

Make up your own based on any strange fact you remember. The weirder, the better!

🐰 BONUS CHALLENGE 🐰
STRANGE BUT REAL? – CAN YOU FOOL A FRIEND?

Try this quick game with a family member or friend!

1. Pick **two strange facts from** this chapter.
2. Then **make up one** totally bizarre fact of your own.
3. Read all three out loud—**in any order.**
4. See if they can guess **which one is fake!**

Example:

- *Napoleon was once attacked by rabbits.*
- *A war started over a wooden bucket.*
- *A chicken ruled ancient Egypt.*

Can they spot the fake? Try switching roles and see who's the best history trickster!

MYTHS, MYSTERIES AND THE UNKNOWN

CHAPTER 17: DIGGING UP THE PAST – FOSSILS, TREASURE HUNTS AND ANCIENT SECRETS

What if the most exciting treasure hunt wasn't in the future—but underground, hidden in the dirt beneath your feet? All over the world, people have uncovered dinosaur bones, ancient tombs, long-lost cities, and even real buried treasure. And the best part? These discoveries aren't just for scientists—some were found by kids, farmers, or everyday explorers who just happened to be looking in the right place.

Fossils help us understand animals that went extinct millions of years ago. Ancient tombs reveal what kings and queens were buried with—and what they believed would follow them into the afterlife. And sometimes, metal detectors lead to sparkling coins and golden helmets buried for centuries.

So grab your shovel (or your curiosity) and get ready to dig into some of the most amazing things ever found underground!

———————— 🦖 🦖 🦖 ————————

TREASURE SHIPS LOST AT SEA

Some of the world's richest treasure is still underwater. In 2015, divers off the coast of Colombia discovered the long-lost Spanish galleon *San José*. It sank in 1708, carrying more than 200 tons of gold, silver, and emeralds, a massive treasure worth over $17 billion today.

Spain, Colombia, salvage companies, and even indigenous groups all claimed ownership, but so far, no one has been allowed to recover the treasure. It's still sitting under the sea—**the richest sunken treasure in history, just out of reach.**

Shipwrecks like this are being found all the time: some with sunken cannons, jeweled goblets, or mysterious cargo. It makes you wonder: how many secrets are still sleeping at the bottom of the sea?

———————— 🦖 🦖 🦖 ————————

THE VIKING SWORD WITH A SECRET CODE

In 2017, archaeologists in Norway uncovered a mysterious Viking sword engraved with unusual markings. At first, it looked like just another artifact—but then experts realized the strange runes might form **a coded message** or even a treasure map.

The sword's symbols don't match typical Viking writing. Some scholars think it could lead to a hidden hoard or mark the identity of a lost warrior. Others believe it was meant to confuse grave robbers or honor a fallen leader in a secret way. No one has cracked the code, yet.

———————————— 🦕 🦕 🦕 ————————————

AMBER: NATURE'S TIME CAPSULE

Amber is hardened tree resin that's been around for millions of years. Sometimes it traps bugs, seeds (even tiny feathers) and preserves them perfectly.

One of the coolest finds? A 100-million-year-old piece of amber from Myanmar that held part of a feathered dinosaur's tail. You could see the tiny bones, muscles, and even the color of the feathers!

It's like nature's sticky camera, freezing a moment in time for us to study millions of years later.

———————————— 🦕 🦕 🦕 ————————————

THE SUTTON HOO HELMET

In 1939, a woman in England hired an amateur archaeologist to investigate some odd mounds on her property. What he found became one of the most important discoveries in British history.

The **Sutton Hoo ship** burial was packed with golden treasures, weapons, and an ornate warrior's helmet—all from the 600s CE. It may have belonged to a king or noble, buried in a ship under a giant mound.

It's like a real-life version of a Viking treasure chest, only buried on land.

———————————— 🦕 🦕 🦕 ————————————

ANCIENT BATTERIES? – THE SHOCKING BAGHDAD DISCOVERY

In the 1930s, archaeologists digging near Baghdad, Iraq, found something strange: a small clay jar with a copper cylinder and iron rod inside. Some scientists believe this was more than just pottery—it might have been an ancient battery.

How would that work? The pieces could have generated a tiny electric current if filled with acidic liquid like vinegar or lemon juice. That's right: electricity, 2,000 years before batteries were officially invented!

Known as the **Baghdad Battery**, it's sparked fierce debate. Was it used for electroplating gold, healing rituals, or something we still don't understand? No one knows for sure, but it's one of the strangest and most electrifying mysteries in archaeology.

THE WHALE THAT WALKED ON LAND

Believe it or not, the ancestors of whales once walked on land! In 2000, scientists in Pakistan found a fossil of a creature called Pakicetus. It had legs, a long tail, and a head like a wolf, but it lived partly in water.

It's one of the weirdest fossils ever found because it proves whales started out as land mammals before returning to the sea.

Can you imagine a whale with legs? It really happened.

DINO POOP HOLDS ANCIENT CLUES

Yes, scientists really do study fossilized dinosaur poop, known as **coprolites**, and they've found some pretty awesome stuff inside.

One fossil revealed that a dino had eaten a tiny lizard with bones still inside, while another contained crushed plant matter and ancient seeds. Coprolites help paleontologists understand dino diets, habitats, and even ecosystems.

It may sound gross, but this ancient poo is a gold mine of prehistoric information!

POMPEII'S SNACK BARS

The ancient Roman city of Pompeii, buried in volcanic ash in 79 CE, is famous for preserving homes, streets... and even restaurants! Over 80 snack bars called **thermopolia** have been discovered there.

One still had painted menus and animal bones inside pots, including duck, goat, and fish! Ancient Romans grabbed a quick bite here, just like we visit food trucks or cafés.

Frozen in time, Pompeii shows that fast food isn't so modern after all.

THE LOST CITY BENEATH THE WAVES

Off the coast of southern Greece, lies the ancient city of **Pavlopetri**, but you won't find it on any land maps. That's because the city sits entirely underwater.

It sank over 5,000 years ago and remained hidden until divers rediscovered it in the 1960s.

Amazingly, the streets, houses, courtyards, and even a plumbing system are still visible. Pavlopetri is believed to be the **oldest known underwater city** in the world, and it shows signs of careful city planning long before modern blueprints ever existed.

Scientists think rising sea levels or a powerful earthquake might have submerged it. Today, Pavlopetri is protected by UNESCO—and you can literally swim through history if you visit with a diving team!

———————————————— 🦕🦕🦕 ————————————————

THE DINOSAUR MUMMY – A FOSSIL WITH SKIN!

Most dinosaur fossils are just bones, but in 2011, paleontologists in Canada made a jaw-dropping discovery: the fossil of a **nodosaur** that still had **armor plates, scaly skin, and even its stomach contents!**

This plant-eating dino, later named **Borealopelta**, was over 110 million years old. What makes it truly incredible is how perfectly it was preserved. Unlike dusty bones, it looks like a statue, or like it simply fell asleep and turned to stone.

Even the dinosaur's skin color was visible! It had reddish-brown camouflage, suggesting it used its body color to blend into the forest. This "dinosaur mummy" is one of the most detailed fossils ever found, and it completely changed how we imagine prehistoric creatures looked in real life.

———————————————— 🦕🦕🦕 ————————————————

THE MUMMY WITH A GOLDEN TONGUE

In 2021, archaeologists in Egypt uncovered something truly bizarre: a 2,000-year-old mummy with **a gold foil tongue!**

The body was buried in a crumbling temple. Experts believe the golden tongue was meant to help the person speak in the afterlife. In ancient Egyptian beliefs, being able to talk to gods was super important.

Who knew a shiny tongue could be a VIP pass to the next world?

———————————————— 🦕🦕🦕 ————————————————

THE ROMAN CURSE TABLETS – TINY SCROLLS OF SPITE

At a Roman temple site in Bath, England, archaeologists discovered a small **lead tablet** buried deep inside an ancient spring. Scratched into its surface was the name of a suspected thief, along with a message **cursing** them and asking the gods to punish them!

People in ancient Rome believed sacred places could carry their messages to the gods. Angry citizens would write curses on metal, then toss them into the water hoping for divine justice. The messages were often addressed to gods, asking for justice, or revenge. One person cursed whoever stole their gloves. Another wanted a thief to "lose their mind and eyes" unless their stolen goods were returned.

These tablets are more than just spooky notes. They offer a rare glimpse into everyday Roman life: the worries, superstitions, and ancient version of "reporting a crime" to the gods. Even today, some of them remain undeciphered, their curses still waiting to be read.

━━━━━━━━━━━━━━ 🐢🐢🐢 ━━━━━━━━━━━━━━

THE TERRACOTTA ARMY GUARDING A DEAD EMPEROR

In 1974, a group of farmers digging a well in China found pieces of pottery underground. But these weren't ordinary pots: they were parts of life-size statues!

They had discovered the **Terracotta Army**, built over 2,000 years ago to guard the tomb of China's first emperor, Qin Shi Huang. So far, more than 8,000 soldier statues have been found, each with a different face, along with horses, chariots, and weapons.

Imagine digging in your backyard and hitting an ancient army!

━━━━━━━━━━━━━━ 🐢🐢🐢 ━━━━━━━━━━━━━━

THE SECRET DOOR IN A PYRAMID

The **Great Pyramid of Giza** has been studied for centuries, but it's still hiding secrets. In 2002, scientists used tiny robots to explore the narrow shafts that branch off from the Queen's Chamber. Deep inside one of them, the robot hit something unexpected: a sealed stone door with metal handles. Behind it? No one knew.

In 2011, a newer robot peered even farther in, only to find yet another mysterious door. And in 2017, scientists using special scanning technology discovered an entire hidden chamber the size of a bus high above the Grand Gallery.

Even today, that space remains unopened. Some believe it could be a secret burial chamber, a structural feature, or something entirely unknown. After more than 4,500 years, the pyramid is still holding on to some of its greatest mysteries, sealed behind ancient stone.

QUIZ:
CAN YOU UNEARTH THE TRUTH?

1) What do scientists think the symbols on the Viking sword might be?

A) A poem

B) A shopping list

C) A secret code or map

2) What was preserved in the piece of amber from Myanmar?

A) A tiny dinosaur tail

B) A gold coin

C) A chameleon tongue

3) Why did ancient Egyptians give a mummy a golden tongue?

A) To scare grave robbers

B) To help them speak in the afterlife

C) As a sign of royalty

4) Where was the Terracotta Army found?

A) Beneath a temple in Rome

B) In a well in China

C) On top of a volcano

5) What strange item was discovered in a Roman spring in Bath, England?

A) A golden ring

B) A curse tablet

C) A map of the stars

Answers: 1-C, 2-A, 3-B, 4-B, 5-B

🔍 TRY THIS! 🔍
CREATE A SECRET DIG SITE

Ready to become a backyard archaeologist?

Grab a small container (like a bowl, box, or plastic bin) and fill it with sand, dirt, or even rice.

Now hide 3–5 small objects inside—coins, toy bones, buttons, or "ancient" paper scrolls.

Your challenge:

1. Invite someone to excavate your site using a spoon or brush
2. Have them describe each item and guess what it was used for
3. Make it tricky by adding fake "mystery objects" or creating a theme—like a pirate hoard or lost city tools

Label your site like a real archaeologist would:

"Site #17 – Temple Ruins, 2024 CE"

🗺️BONUS CHALLENGE🗺️
TREASURE MAP MYSTERY

Time to create your own legendary lost treasure!

Draw a detailed treasure map that leads to a real or imaginary location.

Include:

- Winding paths, rivers, caves, or traps
- Symbols and riddles instead of place names
- A big red X to mark the spot

Now challenge a friend, sibling, or parent to follow your clues. What they find doesn't have to be gold—it could be a silly prize or secret message!

Add a plot twist—maybe the treasure is cursed, or it's just a decoy!

CHAPTER 18: MYTHICAL BEASTS AND LEGENDARY CREATURES – WHAT'S REAL, WHAT'S NOT?

Have you ever heard of a dragon? A unicorn? A creature so strange it had to be made up? Mythical beasts are part of stories told all over the world, but what if some weren't totally imaginary?

Some legendary creatures turned out to be real animals. Others were inspired by ancient bones, strange sightings, or pure imagination. And a few? They're still unproven. No one has ever caught a Bigfoot, but plenty of people say they've seen one.

This chapter explores the blurry line between real and unreal—the creatures we invented, misunderstood, or maybe haven't discovered yet.

―――――――――― 🦄 🦄 🦄 ――――――――――

THE UNICORN'S UNEXPECTED ORIGIN

Unicorns may be magical in fairy tales, but their myth likely started with something real: the **Indian rhinoceros**. Ancient travelers described a huge animal with one horn, tough skin, and a wild temper.

Add a little exaggeration, and soon the world believed in a beautiful horse with a spiral horn that could purify water and heal the sick. Medieval artists even drew unicorns based on second-hand descriptions, often including goat beards and lion tails.

One famous "unicorn horn" was actually a narwhal tusk from the Arctic. Oops!

―――――――――― 🦄 🦄 🦄 ――――――――――

DRAGONS FROM THE BONES OF GIANTS

The idea of dragons appears in almost every ancient culture: China, Europe, the Middle East, and beyond. But where did the stories come from?

One theory: people discovered **dinosaur fossils** long before they knew about extinction or paleontology. Giant bones, sharp teeth, and claws could easily be mistaken for a dragon's remains.

Some fossils in China were even labeled "dragon bones" and ground into powders for medicine. Not fire-breathing, but definitely fierce.

THE KRAKEN AND THE GIANT SQUID

Sailors once told terrifying tales of the **kraken**, a sea monster so big it could sink a ship with its tentacles.

For centuries, scientists thought it was all nonsense, until they discovered the giant squid, a deep-sea creature that can grow over 40 feet long and has eyes the size of dinner plates.

We now know these squids are real. They live in the deep ocean and are rarely seen, but modern submersibles have caught them on camera.

The kraken wasn't completely made up—it just needed a name change.

🦄 🦄 🦄

PHOENIX RISING – THE BIRD THAT BURNS AND IS REBORN

The **phoenix** is one of the most famous mythical creatures of all time: a majestic bird that bursts into flames when it dies... and then rises again from its own ashes.

Stories of the phoenix appear in ancient Egypt, Greece, Rome, and China. In some tales, it sings a beautiful song before it goes up in fire, and then returns even stronger than before.

The phoenix is often a symbol of hope and renewal, and while no bird really explodes and comes back, some real animals (like certain frogs, jellyfish, or lizards) can regrow body parts or survive freezing. Nature's way of saying: the myth isn't that far off!

🦄 🦄 🦄

MERMAIDS AND MANATEES

When sailors spotted manatees or dugongs from their ships, they sometimes mistook them for **mermaids**: half-human, half-fish beings with flowing hair.

It sounds silly today, but long sea voyages and blurry distances led to all kinds of wild guesses. Even **Christopher Columbus** recorded seeing mermaids (though he admitted they were "not as beautiful as legend says").

Sea cows may not sing or hold tridents, but they do explain a legendary mix-up.

🦄 🦄 🦄

THE REAL-LIFE HOBBITS OF INDONESIA

In 2003, scientists discovered skeletons of tiny humans on the Indonesian island of Flores. Nicknamed **hobbits** (like the ones from The Lord of the Rings), these people stood just 3 feet tall and lived about 50,000 years ago.

They're officially called Homo floresiensis, and they may have coexisted with early modern humans.

Legends from the island describe small forest people who were shy, quick, and clever. Sound familiar?

————————————— 🦄 🦄 🦄 —————————————

THE GRIFFIN AND THE DINO-BIRD CONFUSION

The **griffin**—a beast with the body of a lion and the head and wings of an eagle—has roots in ancient Greek and Scythian art.

Some experts believe the idea came from **Protoceratops fossils** found in Central Asia. These beaked dinosaurs had large heads and clawed limbs, and their bones often appeared near gold mines.

What better way to guard treasure than with a fossil-inspired guardian?

————————————— 🦄 🦄 🦄 —————————————

BIGFOOT AND THE FOREST SHADOWS

North America's best-known mythical creature is **Bigfoot**, also called Sasquatch: a tall, hairy, human-like beast that roams the woods.

Photos, videos, and footprints have been collected for decades, but no one has ever found real evidence like bones or fur. Could it be a bear standing upright? A hoax? Or is Bigfoot just really good at hiding?

The mystery is part of the fun.

————————————— 🦄 🦄 🦄 —————————————

THE MONGOLIAN DEATH WORM

Said to lurk in the Gobi Desert, the **Mongolian Death Worm** is a legendary red creature that can kill with electric shocks or poisonous spit. While no one has ever caught one, locals believe it hides beneath the sand, surfacing during storms.

Scientists think the myth may be based on sightings of real desert reptiles (like snakes or legless lizards) but no solid proof has emerged. Just because it's not proven doesn't mean it isn't scary!

Some fans believe the **Mongolian Death Worm** inspired the deadly sand-worms in Dune. Though author Frank Herbert never confirmed it, the idea of a mysterious, desert-dwelling monster with hidden powers feels like more than coincidence!

THE CHUPACABRA AND THE MYSTERY OF MANGY COYOTES

In Latin American folklore, the **chupacabra** is a blood-sucking beast that attacks goats and livestock.

Reports in the 1990s described it as a reptile-like creature with spines down its back, but later sightings in the U.S. turned out to be **coyotes or wild dogs** with a skin disease called mange.

Hairless, scabby, and spooky, these sick animals looked so strange that people assumed they were something supernatural. Sometimes nature just gets weird.

THE LOCH NESS MONSTER – TRUTH BENEATH THE SURFACE?

The legend of the **Loch Ness Monster**, or "Nessie," began in Scotland in the 1930s, when a photo showed a long-necked shape rising from the lake. Some thought it was a sea serpent. Others said it was a dinosaur that never went extinct.

Over the years, people have claimed to see humps, wakes, and shadows in the water. Scientists have scanned the lake with sonar and drones, but found no monster, just fish, eels, and logs.

Still, the mystery lives on. Could Nessie be a hoax, a misidentification, or something science hasn't found yet?

THE BASILISK AND THE DEADLY COBRA STARE

The **basilisk** was said to kill with a single look. It appeared in European legends as a snake or dragon that could cause death with its gaze.

While that's a stretch, cobras and other venomous snakes **do lift their heads**, flare hoods, and maintain **unblinking eye contact** before striking.

The idea of a deadly stare may have started with a very real reptilian warning.

THUNDERBIRDS AND THE WINGSPAN OF WONDER

Native American legends tell of **thunderbirds**: giant birds with wings so big they made thunder when flapped and lightning shot from its eyes. These stories likely came from real sightings of massive prehistoric birds or even distant views of large eagles like giant condors.

One fossil bird, *Argentavis*, had a wingspan over 23 feet—the size of a small airplane! If something that big flew overhead, you might hear thunder too.

— 🐎 🐎 🐎 —

CHIMERAS AND HYBRID CREATURES – MIXED-UP MONSTERS

Imagine a creature with the head of a lion, the body of a goat, and the tail of a snake—all rolled into one! That's the **Chimera**, a legendary monster from Greek mythology. It was said to breathe fire and cause chaos wherever it went.

Many ancient cultures had similar "hybrid beasts": the **sphinx**, the **manticore**, or the **griffin**. Some may have come from creative storytelling, others from seeing real animals and mixing up their features.

Today, hybrid animals do exist—like the *liger* (lion + tiger) or *zonkey* (zebra + donkey). And scientists are even experimenting with creating chimeras in the lab (don't worry, not the fire-breathing kind!). Sometimes, myth meets biology in the strangest ways.

— 🐎 🐎 🐎 —

THE BUNYIP AND THE SECRETS OF THE BILLABONG

From Australian Aboriginal folklore comes the Bunyip, a mysterious creature said to live in murky lakes and billabongs. Stories described it as anything from a giant dog-faced sea monster to a duck-billed beast with flippers and tusks.

No one ever agreed on what the Bunyip looked like, but everyone agreed you didn't want to meet one. Early settlers were so spooked by the legends that they searched swamps for bones and even claimed to hear terrifying roars at night.

What inspired the myth? Some think early sightings of now-extinct megafauna like giant wombats may have played a role. Others say... it's still out there, hiding in the reeds.

🧠QUIZ:🧠
REAL, FAKE, OR IN BETWEEN?

1) Which sea monster likely came from sightings of giant squid?

A) Leviathan

B) Kraken

C) Basilisk

2) What animal helped create the myth of mermaids?

A) Swordfish

B) Otters

C) Manatees

3) What condition might have inspired werewolf myths?

A) Hypertrichosis

B) Hypnosis

C) Hydrophobia

4) What creature is thought to be inspired by dinosaur bones?

A) Unicorn

B) Griffin

C) Bigfoot

5) Where were "real-life hobbits" discovered?

A) Australia

B) Indonesia

C) Madagascar

Answers: 1-B, 2-C, 3-A, 4-B, 5-B

🐴 TRY THIS! 🐴
MYTHICAL BEAST BUILDER

Forget just drawing—**build** your creature! Use craft supplies, toys, recycled materials, or even snacks to create a 3D mythical beast. **Steps**:

- Combine parts from different animals (real or legendary): wings, hooves, horns, tentacles—you name it!
- Give your creature a name, a backstory, and a special power
- Present it as if you're unveiling a discovery in a museum

Create a "warning label" for your beast: *"Caution: Shoots rainbow fire when startled!"*

🐾 BONUS CHALLENGE 🐾
CREATURE TRACKER FIELD MISSION

Turn your space into a mythical creature tracking zone! Your mission:

- Pick a mythical beast from the chapter
- Leave behind "evidence" of its presence—footprints (drawn or made from cut-outs), fur tufts (yarn or cotton), claw marks (paper scratches), or mysterious sounds (use your voice!)
- Challenge someone to follow the clues and identify which creature visited

Create a creature "trap" or hiding place and see if they can find where it lives!

CHAPTER 19: UNSOLVED MYSTERIES – SCIENCE CAN'T EXPLAIN EVERYTHING!

We live in a world filled with answers. We can measure the temperature on Mars, track hurricanes from space, and explain why soda fizzes. Science is amazing!

But... it doesn't know everything.

Some things in our universe are still puzzling, even to the smartest scientists. Glowing balls of lightning? A 500-year-old book no one can read? A river that swallows water and never gives it back?

In this chapter, we'll explore puzzles that make experts scratch their heads, raise their eyebrows, and say, "We're still working on that." Just because we don't have an answer yet doesn't mean there isn't one. It just means someone—maybe even you—hasn't solved it yet.

🔍 🔍 🔍

THE BERMUDA TRIANGLE

The area between Florida, Bermuda, and Puerto Rico has gained fame for being the site of many unexplained disappearances: ships, planes, and even crews have vanished.

For decades, sailors and pilots have told stories of compasses going wild, radio signals vanishing, and even thick fog that seems to swallow everything. Some say it's magnetic forces, others blame sea monsters, whirlpools, or even underwater alien bases!

Scientists believe most disappearances have natural explanations like storms or human error, but still, over 1,000 incidents have been linked to the area. The ocean keeps its secrets... and this triangle may be the most mysterious patch of water on Earth.

🔍 🔍 🔍

THE SECRET LIFE OF EELS

Eels live in rivers and lakes, but when it's time to reproduce, they vanish, traveling thousands of miles to the **Sargasso Sea** in the middle of the Atlantic Ocean.

But no one has ever seen exactly how or where eels spawn. Baby eels appear in the sea and slowly return to freshwater... but the adults? They're still a mystery. After centuries of study, even modern science hasn't figured out the full story of how eels reproduce.

— 🔍 🔍 🔍 —

THE TUNGUSKA BOOM

In 1908, something exploded in the sky over Siberia, flattening over 800 square miles of forest. Trees were knocked over like matchsticks. People felt the shock-wave hundreds of miles away.

No crater was found. Most scientists believe a comet or asteroid exploded in the atmosphere, but there was no impact site, and no fragments were ever recovered.

What really caused the Tunguska Event? Over 100 years later, we still don't know for sure.

— 🔍 🔍 🔍 —

LIGHTNING THAT ROLLS LIKE A BALL

Most lightning strikes are loud, fast, and zigzag across the sky. But **ball lightning** is different—and it's still unexplained.

Witnesses have seen glowing spheres float through the air during storms, drift into rooms, or even roll down chimneys. Some vanish silently. Others explode!

Scientists have tried to recreate ball lightning in labs with limited success. Is it plasma? A hallucination? Some kind of electric fog? No one knows for sure.

— 🔍 🔍 🔍 —

THE SAILING STONES OF DEATH VALLEY

In California's Death Valley, rocks as big as bowling balls move mysteriously across the desert floor—**leaving trails behind them**, even though no one sees them move.

For decades, no one knew how this happened. There's no wind strong enough. No people around. No footprints. Nothing.

The best theory so far? A thin layer of ice forms under the rocks at night and is pushed by very light winds. But it still hasn't been fully observed in action, making these wandering rocks one of nature's coolest unsolved riddles.

THE RIVER THAT EATS ITSELF

In northern Minnesota, part of the Brule River disappears into a giant hole known as **The Devil's Kettle.** Scientists have poured dye, balls, and even GPS trackers into the hole to find out where the water goes.

None have been found. Some believe the water flows into hidden underground tunnels or caverns, but no one has ever followed its path. It's one of **the weirdest hydrological mysteries** in North America.

THE GREAT CORAL WHISPER

Coral reefs are like underwater cities: full of color, movement, and life. But scientists have discovered something totally unexpected: some coral may **communicate using sound.**

In certain reefs, researchers have recorded strange clicking or popping noises that seem to attract fish larvae and influence coral behavior. Are they messages? Navigation signals? Just weird side effects of tiny movements?

No one knows for sure. We still don't fully understand how coral reefs "talk."

BOOKS NO ONE CAN READ

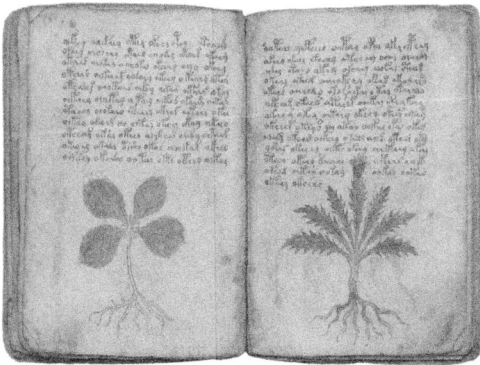

Imagine finding a book filled with illustrations of strange plants and diagrams of stars, but written in a language no one understands. That's the **Voynich Manuscript,** a 500-year-old book that has never been decoded. Its alphabet doesn't match any known language, and even computers can't crack it.

Now add the **Codex Seraphinianus,** created in the 1980s. It's full of weird machines, impossible creatures, and made-up symbols—but the author says it's not meant to be read at all. It's art. Or maybe... it's a mystery too?

These books may not share an origin, but they share something else: no one can read them—and no one is quite sure why they exist.

BEES CAN DO MATH?

Here's a mystery no one saw coming: bees might understand numbers.

In lab tests, bees were trained to choose between images with more or fewer shapes, and they got it right. Some even showed signs of basic addition and subtraction!

How can an insect with a brain the size of a poppy seed do math? What's happening inside that tiny buzzing head? Scientists are still trying to figure it out.

WHAT'S REALLY AT EARTH'S CORE?

We know the Earth has layers, but **the inner core** remains a big mystery.

It's too deep to reach with any machine, and most of what we know comes from studying earthquakes. Some scientists think the core rotates differently than the rest of the planet. Others believe it's changing shape.

Until we can drill 4,000 miles down (don't hold your breath), we're just guessing.

THE ANTIKYTHERA MECHANISM – A COMPUTER FROM ANCIENT GREECE?

In 1901, divers exploring a shipwreck off the coast of Greece, found something strange: a lump of corroded bronze gears. For decades, people didn't know what it was, until scientists realized it was **an ancient mechanical computer**, over 2,000 years old!

Now known as the **Antikythera Mechanism**, it could predict eclipses, track the positions of the planets, and even calculate the dates of the Olympic Games. It had dozens of tiny gears, all hand-cut with incredible precision. But here's the mystery: no other machine like it existed for more than 1,000 years. Scientists call it the world's first computer, built long before such tech was thought possible. Who made it? How did they build it? We still don't know.

It's a real artifact from ancient Greece that still puzzles modern engineers: it proves that the ancients were a lot more high-tech than we thought.

THE GREEN CHILDREN OF WOOLPIT – VISITORS FROM BELOW?

In the 1100s, villagers in Woolpit, England, got a shock. Two strange children appeared near a wolf trap: **a boy and a girl with green skin**. They wore odd clothes, spoke a language no one understood, and seemed terrified of sunlight.

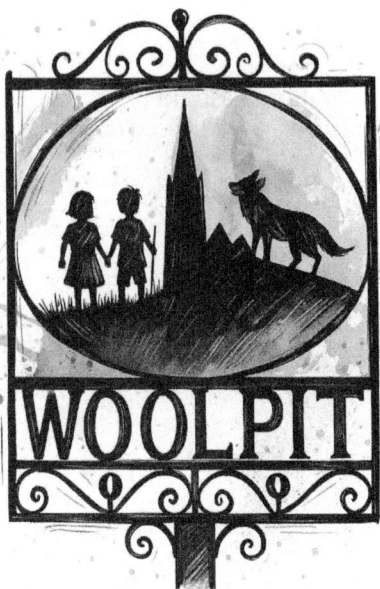

At first, they refused all food except raw beans. Eventually, the girl adapted—she learned English and began to eat normally. But the boy grew sick and died. When asked where they came from, the girl said they were from a place called **"St. Martin's Land,"** a twilight world underground where everyone was green and it was always dusk. She claimed they'd gotten lost while tending their father's cattle and wandered into the light.

Historians have tried to explain the tale for centuries. Was it a garbled folk story? A misunderstood illness like anemia? Or did something really strange happen in Woolpit? No one knows the truth—but the green children's story is still one of the weirdest tales in English history.

THE NAZCA LINES – MESSAGES FOR THE SKY?

In the deserts of Peru, there's a giant outdoor mystery: massive shapes etched into the ground, called the Nazca Lines. Some look like monkeys, spiders, hummingbirds, and other animals. Others are geometric shapes, zigzags, or spirals. Some stretch longer than a football field!

But here's the wild part: they were made over 1,500 years ago, and they're so big that you can really only see them from the air. And yet, the Nazca people had no airplanes or satellites. So... how did they make them so perfectly?

No one knows exactly why they were created. Were they messages to the gods? Star maps? Walking paths for rituals? Or... were they built for someone (or something) watching from above? Scientists, historians, and even pilots still debate their purpose.

QUIZ:
UNSOLVED MYSTERIES

1) What's strange about the Voynich Manuscript?

A) It's blank

B) It's in a made-up language no one can read

C) It predicts the future

2) What part of the Earth is still mostly a mystery?

A) The oceans

B) The mountains

C) The inner core

3) Where do eels go to spawn?

A) The Amazon River

B) The Sargasso Sea

C) Nowhere—they don't spawn!

4) Which mysterious place was said to be always in twilight, with people who had green skin?

A) Atlantis

B) St. Martin's Land

C) Shangri-La

5) What did scientists discover about bees?

A) They can fly to the Moon

B) They make honey glow in the dark

C) They might understand numbers

Answers: 1-B, 2-C, 3-B, 4-B, 5-C

🕵️ TRY THIS! 🕵️
THINK LIKE A THEORIST

Pick one of the mysteries from this chapter—then come up with your own theory to explain it!

- Why do you think eels are so hard to study?
- Could the boiling river be hiding something deep underground?
- How do bees do math with such tiny brains?

Write 2–3 sentences or draw a diagram showing your idea. Be creative—just back it up with logic (even if it's wild!).

Bonus: Share your theory with a friend or family member and ask if they believe it!

📜 BONUS CHALLENGE 📜
UNCRACKABLE MYSTERY FILE

Every great scientist needs a case file! Choose your favorite mystery from this chapter and create your own top-secret investigation folder.

Here's how:

1. Make a two-column chart:
   - Left column: "What We Know" — list the facts and clues
   - Right column: "What We Don't Know" — list the questions or gaps
2. Draw a small sketch or symbol that represents your mystery (like a lightning ball, strange book, or signal wave).

At the bottom of your file, write your own theory to explain the mystery. Try to connect it to real science—but don't be afraid to think outside the box!

CHAPTER 20: VANISHED CIVILIZATIONS – LOST WORLDS OF THE PAST

Throughout history, great civilizations rose to power, built stunning cities, invented incredible things—and then completely disappeared. Some left behind massive temples, strange writings, or mysterious statues. Others left barely a trace at all.

Why did they vanish? Was it war? Drought? Disease? Climate change? Or something we still haven't figured out?

In this chapter, you'll explore lost worlds and forgotten peoples: civilizations that once thrived and then faded into legend. Many of their secrets remain buried, waiting to be discovered.

──────────── 🪨🪨🪨 ────────────

THE RAPA NUI – BUILDERS OF EASTER ISLAND

Far out in the Pacific Ocean lies **Easter Island**, famous for its massive stone statues known as **moai**. These were created by the **Rapa Nui** people, who lived in extreme isolation for centuries.

They carved nearly 900 moai—some over 30 feet tall—and moved them across the island using unknown methods. How they transported these massive stone figures remains a mystery.

Over time, their society declined, possibly due to deforestation, overuse of resources, or outside contact. Today, the moai still stand, silent sentinels of a once-thriving culture.

──────────── 🪨🪨🪨 ────────────

CAHOKIA – AMERICA'S FORGOTTEN CITY

Before Columbus arrived, a huge city called **Cahokia** stood near today's St. Louis, Missouri. Around 1100 CE, it had tens of thousands of people: more than London at the time!

The city was filled with huge earthen mounds, wide plazas, and wooden temples. The biggest mound, called **Monks Mound,** is 100 feet tall and still stands today. But by 1400, Cahokia was mysteriously abandoned. No one knows exactly why—maybe war, drought, or disease. For centuries, few people even knew it existed.

Many people in the U.S. have never heard of Cahokia, but it was once the heart of a mighty Native American society known as the Mississippian culture.

THE MINOANS – LEGENDS BEHIND ATLANTIS?

The Minoans lived on the island of Crete over 3,000 years ago. They built palaces with plumbing, wrote mysterious symbols, and painted colorful murals. Their largest palace, **Knossos**, may have inspired the famous myth of the **Labyrinth and the Minotaur.**

Then, a giant volcano erupted nearby, one of the biggest in history. Massive tsunamis and shaking ground may have destroyed cities and weakened their empire.

Some believe the Minoans were the real **Atlantis**, the advanced island civilization that vanished into the sea. Whether or not that's true, their disappearance remains one of the great mysteries of the ancient world.

——————— 🎲🎲🎲 ———————

THE MAYA – CITIES SWALLOWED BY THE JUNGLE

The **Maya** built huge cities in Central America, complete with pyramids, palaces, and observatories. They had advanced math, calendars, and writing—and then around 900 CE, many of their cities were abandoned.

No one knows exactly why. Theories include drought, war, rebellion, or a combination of problems. Some Maya descendants still live today, but their ancient cities remain covered by forest.

Imagine an entire civilization slowly disappearing beneath the leaves.

——————— 🎲🎲🎲 ———————

GÖBEKLI TEPE – THE TEMPLE THAT CHANGED HISTORY

Long before the pyramids or Stonehenge (about 11,000 years ago) people in present-day Turkey built **Göbekli Tepe**, the world's oldest known temple.

Massive stone pillars with animal carvings were arranged in circles, before farming, metal, or writing even existed! Then, strangely, it was buried on purpose, and the people vanished.

It's so old that it rewrote what we thought we knew about civilization.

——————— 🎲🎲🎲 ———————

THE INDUS VALLEY CIVILIZATION – A SILENT COLLAPSE

Over 4,000 years ago, a vast civilization thrived along the Indus River in what's now Pakistan and northwest India. The **Indus Valley Civilization** built carefully planned cities, complete with straight roads, brick homes, public baths, and even underground drains: a level of cleanliness that wowed archaeologists.

But here's the mystery: they vanished. Their cities, like **Mohenjo-daro** and Harappa, were abandoned, and their writing system has never been decoded. There are no giant palaces or tombs—just a peaceful, puzzling silence.

It's one of history's most peaceful and puzzling disappearances.

———————————— 🧱🧱🧱 ————————————

ANGKOR – THE JUNGLE CITY OF TOWERS

Centuries ago, the **Khmer Empire** built the vast city of **Angkor** in what is now Cambodia, including the famous temple Angkor Wat. At its peak, it was one of the largest cities in the world, filled with grand temples, canals, and towering statues.

But by the 1400s, much of Angkor was mysteriously abandoned. Some believe invading armies or massive droughts may have been the cause. Over time, the jungle grew over the stone buildings, hiding them from the world.

When European explorers stumbled upon Angkor in the 1800s, they couldn't believe such a place existed. Even today, archaeologists are still uncovering lost parts of the city, piece by piece.

———————————— 🧱🧱🧱 ————————————

THE KINGDOM OF AKSUM – VANISHED FROM THE MAP

In ancient Ethiopia, **the Kingdom of Aksum** was a wealthy empire known for tall stone obelisks and early Christianity. It traded with Rome, Persia, and India.

Around the 7th century, it started to decline. Some say climate change ruined crops. Others blame shifting trade routes. Aksum vanished, and for centuries, no one knew it had existed.

———————————— 🧱🧱🧱 ————————————

THE ANCESTRAL PUEBLOANS – CLIFF DWELLERS OF THE SOUTHWEST

In the American Southwest, the **Ancestral Puebloans** (sometimes called the Anasazi) built dramatic cliffside homes like those at **Mesa Verde.**

They created complex societies, farming in dry land using clever techniques. But by the late 1200s, many cliff cities were abandoned.

The reasons? Possibly drought, crop failure, or conflict. Modern Pueblo peoples are their descendants, but much of their early story is a mystery.

———————— 🗿 🗿 🗿 ————————

THE OLMECS – FACES WITH NO NAMES

Before the Maya, the **Olmecs** lived in Mexico and left behind giant stone heads weighing tons—some with helmets, staring into the distance.

But we don't know what they called themselves. We can't read their writing. Their society disappeared around 400 BCE.

Were they the "mother culture" of Mesoamerica? Or just one of many early puzzle pieces?

———————— 🗿 🗿 🗿 ————————

THE MOCHE – PYRAMID BUILDERS OF THE DESERT

Long before the Inca, the **M**oche civilization ruled northern Peru. They built **huge adobe pyramids, i**ncluding one nicknamed the **Huaca del Sol**, or Temple of the Sun.

They were master artists, creating detailed pottery that showed everything from daily life to legends. But sometime around 800 CE, a series of powerful El Niño floods likely destroyed their cities.

Their pyramids still stand, half-buried in desert sands.

———————— 🗿 🗿 🗿 ————————

THE SEA PEOPLES – RAIDERS OF THE BRONZE AGE

Around 1200 BCE, cities all across the Mediterranean were attacked or destroyed. Egypt, Greece, and Turkey were all hit. Who caused this chaos? Ancient texts blame mysterious invaders called the **Sea Peoples.**

No one knows exactly who they were or where they came from. They vanished as quickly as they appeared.

It was like a real-life ancient apocalypse—and no one has cracked the code.

———————— 🗿 🗿 🗿 ————————

THE TARTESSIANS – THE GOLDEN MYSTERY OF SPAIN

More than 2,500 years ago, a wealthy culture called the **Tartessians** lived in southern Spain. Ancient Greeks said they had **rivers of silver and gold,** huge cities, and even kings who wrote poetry.

But suddenly, around 500 BCE—they were gone. Their writing disappeared, their cities vanished, and no one really knows why. Some even link them to the myth of Atlantis.

— 🗿🗿🗿 —

THE LYCIANS – TOMBS IN THE CLIFFS

The **Lycians** lived in what is now Turkey, and their cities were built into cliffs, with elaborate tombs carved high into rock faces.

They had their own language and unique customs but were eventually absorbed by larger empires like Persia and Rome. Their tombs remain, but their story faded.

Stone whispers from a forgotten people.

— 🗿🗿🗿 —

THE GARAMANTES – DESERT KINGS OF THE SAHARA

Deep in the Sahara Desert, the **Garamantes** created an oasis kingdom in what is now southern Libya. From about 500 BCE to 500 CE, they built cities, underground irrigation tunnels called *foggaras*, and even had their own writing system.

They were once seen as simple desert dwellers, but recent archaeology shows they had stone buildings, advanced farming, and traded with Rome and Carthage.

Their civilization eventually vanished—likely due to the desert growing even drier. Today, their cities lie beneath the sand, waiting to be fully uncovered.

— 🗿🗿🗿 —

THE SOGDIANS – TRADERS LOST TO TIME

The **Sogdians** were expert merchants who once ruled trade routes through Central Asia, connecting China, Persia, and the Roman Empire via the **Silk Road**. Their cities, like Samarkand and Panjakent, buzzed with cultural exchange, art, and innovation.

They spoke their own language, practiced many religions, and acted as translators between East and West. But over time, shifting trade routes, invasions, and cultural blending caused their distinct identity to fade.

QUIZ:
LOST, FOUND, OR STILL UNKNOWN?

1) Which ancient civilization built the palace of Knossos and may have inspired the legend of Atlantis?

A) Minoans

B) Olmecs

C) Lycians

2) The giant stone heads left behind in Mexico were created by whom?

A) Maya

B) Sea Peoples

C) Olmecs

3) Which ancient civilization in South Asia had working plumbing?

A) Aksum

B) Indus Valley

C) Rapa Nui

4) What vanished city was larger than London in its time?

A) Petra

B) Cahokia

C) Kandovan

5) Who were the mysterious invaders of the ancient Mediterranean?

A) Lycians

B) Puebloans

C) Sea Peoples

Answers: 1-A, 2-C, 3-B, 4-B, 5-C

🗿 TRY THIS! 🗿
BUILD YOUR LOST CIVILIZATION

Time to bring an ancient world back to life—your way!

Use blocks, LEGOs, clay, cardboard, or any craft supplies to build part of a long-lost civilization.

Will you create a giant temple? A spiral city? A pyramid with a secret tunnel?

Give your structures names and invent their purpose: *"The Sky Gate was only opened once every 100 years..."*

Add something mysterious—like **a glowing stone, vanishing door, or strange writing no one can read.**

⌛ BONUS CHALLENGE ⌛
SOLVE THE ANCIENT MYSTERY

You're an archaeologist on the edge of a major discovery—but you'll need to crack the code first!

Your mission:

1. Make 3 clues using symbols, riddles, or drawings
2. Hide a small "treasure" (a toy, note, or surprise) somewhere in your home
3. Give your clues to a friend or family member and see if they can solve the mystery!

Add a challenge—can they escape a "trap" or pass a "test" before reaching the final clue?

CERTIFICATE OF COMPLETION

This is to proudly certify that

_____

has explored every chapter of
Seriously Fun Facts for Curious Kids
and has earned the title of:

**Master of
Mind-Blowing Curiosity**

*From deep oceans to outer space...
from ancient ruins to robot chefs...
you've uncovered the world's most astonishing secrets.
A curious mind is one of the most powerful things on Earth.*

Date: ___/ ___/ _____

Adam Coolidge

Dear Reader,

Thank you for exploring Seriously Fun Facts for Curious Kids!

Creating this book has been an incredible journey - and I hope it sparked your curiosity, made you smile, and maybe even made you say, "Wait, is that true?!"

This book was written for young explorers just like you - readers who love to learn weird, wonderful, and totally surprising things about the world. If it made you think, imagine, or wonder more, then my mission is complete.

I'd love to hear what you thought. Your feedback means a lot to me - and it helps others discover Seriously Fun Facts for Curious Kids too!

If you enjoyed it, please consider leaving a quick review online.

Got a favorite fact, a question, or a fun suggestion for a future book?

I'd be thrilled to hear from you!

Email: adamcoolidge.official@gmail.com

Author's page

Write a customer
review

Thanks again—and stay curious!

With appreciation,

Adam Coolidge

Printed in Dunstable, United Kingdom